SOMERSET

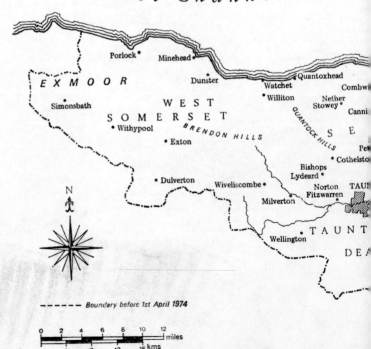

South Wales

Bristol Channel

Flat Holm

Steep Holm

Brear

Porlock

Minehead

EXMOOR

Dunster

Watchet

Quantoxhead

Combwi

Simonsbath

WEST

Williton

Nether
Stowey

Canni

SOMERSET

Withypool

BRENDON HILLS

QUANTOCK HILLS

S E

Exton

Pet

Cothelsto

Bishops
Lydeard

Dulverton

Wiveliscombe

Norton
Fitzwarren

TAUN

N

Milverton

T A U N T

Wellington

D E A

Boundary before 1st April 1974

0   2   4   6   8   10   12
                          miles
    4   8   12   16 kms

SOMERSET

Ralph Whitlock

B.T. Batsford Ltd London and Sydney

First published 1975
© Ralph Whitlock 1975
ISBN 0 7134 2905 4

Printed and bound in Great Britain by
Richard Clay (The Chaucer Press) Ltd, Bungay, Suffolk
for the Publishers B. T. Batsford Ltd,
4 Fitzhardinge Street, London W1H 0AH
and 23 Cross Street, Brookvale, N.S.W.2100, Australia

Contents

List of Illustrations

Acknowledgements

The Author and Publishers would like to thank the following for permission to use photographs in this book: Peter Baker Photography (Pl. 1); J. Allan Cash (Pl. 16); A. F. Kersting FRPS (Pls. 2, 3, 4, 5d, 6, 7, 8c & d, 9, 10, 11, 12, 14, 15); Kenneth Scowen FRPS FIIP (Pl. 13); and G. H. E. Young (Pls. 17, 18). Plates 5a–c and 8a are from the Publishers' Collection.

The map of Somerset is by Patrick Leeson.

1. Introduction:
The Old Crooked Shire

The suggested derivations of two of the names for 'the old crooked shire in the West', whether they are valid or not, offer clues to the character of the county. Of the word *Somerset* itself, '*set*' is by one school of thought said to be derived from 'saetan' or 'settlers', while '*Somer*' simply means 'summer'. The implication is that the heartlands of Somerset provided good summer grazing for the flocks and herds of early Saxon settlers, who retreated elsewhere when the winter floods arrived. Other authorities suggest '*Seo-mere-saetan*', meaning 'settlers by the sea lakes', and 'sea-lakes' is indeed a good description of the marshy lagoons that once formed the heartland of Somerset. The name '*Avalon*' is reserved more properly for the former island on which Glastonbury is situated though also applied to a nebulous realm incorporating most of central Somerset. It is supposed to mean 'the land of apples' or 'the apple orchard'.

The picture we get from these words is a warm, sheltered haven of pastures and fruit trees, tucked away in the West, and that is what Somerset is.

The heart of the county is a territory of flat meadows intersected by a maze of slow-flowing rivers, the Tone, Parret, Isle, Brue and all their tributaries. Separating them, and providing contrast in the landscape, are ridges of grey and golden limestone, valued as a source of fine building stone. Around the river basins the hills rise, in some places abruptly and in others in a confused tangle, to a high rim which effectively shuts the 'land of orchards' off from the rest of England, the barrier being particularly effective in the east and north. Somerset turns its back on the aggressive world and, snuggling behind its ramparts, gazes dreamily westwards.

In the north the deep-cut valley of the Avon has, throughout history though less noticeably now, accentuated the county's isolation from its neighbours. Bath itself is a frontier city. Bristol, although in due course it filched a slice of territory from Somerset, originally belonged wholly to Gloucestershire. Commuterdom has occupied much of the territory between these two cities and the Mendips (a territory which is now being incorporated in the new county of Avon), but is fairly effectively halted by that austere, bleak plateau. Similarly, Somerset has been relatively little affected by the human tide which has engulfed most of Hampshire and is spilling over into Wiltshire and Dorset from the direction of London. Attempting to travel along the main roads of Somerset on summer week-ends has become a penance and a nightmare, but at least the cars are mostly on their way to seaside destinations beyond the county limits. Whether that will change when the M5 extends its probing tentacle southwards from Bristol to Exeter remains to be seen, but, for the present, away from the featureless highways Somerset retains much of its ancient peace.

It has, of course, holiday resorts of its own. On the coast Weston-super-Mare and Minehead attract a share of the crowds, and Cheddar tends to be painfully congested during much of the summer. Bath, too, is on the visiting list of most foreign tourists. Somerset's million acres can, however, absorb many more than its present quota of visitors without sinking beneath their weight. Minehead in particular, with its popular Butlin's holiday complex, is flanked by the lonely heights of Exmoor and the Brendon Hills, where a man may wander all day with only the curlews and crows for company and get lost in the process.

Geologically, Somerset lies west of the broad belt of uncomplicated measures, such as the chalk and limestone, which extend diagonally, from south-west to north-east, across England. Here the strata are much more complex. The hills of the west (Exmoor, the Brendons and the Quantocks) are sandstone; the great arc of hills from south of Taunton to Bath are limestone. Between lie Keuper beds and extensive alluvial flats. The Mendips are an island of carboniferous limestone; and there are several pockets of coal measures, notably around Radstock.

Somerset's newest land was acquired within historical times. Meare Lake Village, just over a mile from Glastonbury, was founded in the third century B.C., on an artificial island. The greater part of the Somerset levels were then a maze of pools and connecting channels, with occasional islands and mud-banks to add to the confusion. Shallow-draught boats could, if guided by a local pilot, penetrate by water into the heart of Somerset. Meare Pool, in which the lake village was built on stilts, was one of the last remnants of the aquatic past to be won for plough and pasture, having been reclaimed in the seventeenth century. Behind this final episode stretched long centuries of patient reclamation work, much of it at the instigation of the Abbots of Glastonbury. Even now, it is easy for the unstable plain to relapse. As recently as February 1974, while this book was being written, floods after weeks of heavy rain turned most of central Somerset into a muddy lake, studded with islets and forlorn willows.

The creation of Meare Lake Village seems to have coincided with an invasion of Britain by Celts from north-western Europe, though whether the builders were the invaders or refugees from them is not clear. Probably it is futile to speculate, for the Celts seem to have imposed themselves as an aristocracy, lording it over the tribes they found already in possession, while they themselves indulged in internecine warfare. To this age belong the hill forts, such as the one on Ham Hill and the several Cadbury Castles.

After Vespasian's campaign in the West Country in A.D. 44 and 45, the Roman peace prevailed over Somerset for more than three hundred years. As elsewhere, the local gentry evidently became Romanized. Town and villa life developed and flourished. The slaves who worked the lead-mines of Mendip (which they were doing as early as A.D. 49) would no doubt have had complaints to air if anyone had asked them, but nobody did. A dozen or two villas, which corresponded to our country estates, have been found in Somerset, and probably many more remain to be located. Other traces of the Roman era are numerous.

Extraordinary procrastinations marked the next conquest of Somerset. Following the final withdrawal of Roman garrisons, the fifth century staggered along, with Britain beset by barbarians (Saxons, Picts and Irish) on nearly every side yet retaining a precarious independence. At the end of the century, when the enemy closed in for a final thrust, the Britons found a champion who sent the invaders reeling back in resounding defeat. This was the half-legendary Arthur, whom persistent traditions link with Somerset and notably with Cadbury Castle. We trace his story in Chapters 2 and 5.

After his passing, the Saxon advance was resumed. A battle at Dyrham, in the borders of Wiltshire and Gloucestershire, in 577, opened the way to the invasion of Somerset. Bath fell. Yet seventy years later there is no evidence that they had got any farther. They were held up roughly along the line of Selwood. It was 658 before the Saxons broke through and penetrated into the heart of Somerset.

Even then, the subjugation of the future county was by no means complete. In 682, twenty-four years after the Saxons passed Selwood, they were still fighting Britons on the Poldens. It was not until the year 733 that Somerton was taken. Yet as early as about 680 a Saxon named Winfrith, who afterwards became Saint Boniface, 'the Apostle of Germany', was born at Crediton in Devon, miles beyond the present border of Somerset, and was later educated at a Benedictine monastery at Exeter.

Obviously there was not ceaseless war between Saxon and Celt. A salient point was that the Saxons, during the long check east of Selwood, had become Christian. When they took Glastonbury it is noteworthy that their king, Kenwalch, left the British abbot, Bregored, in office, with a mixed chapter of British and Saxon monks. Ina, one of the great West Saxon kings whose reign began in 688, was a Somerset man by birth.

Contrary, then, to what happened in many other parts of Britain, in Somerset there was no dramatic conquest resulting in the wholesale replacement of one race by another. For two hundred years after the end of the Roman era, Somerset was an integral part of a realm ruled by Celtic kings. Even before that it was predominantly Celtic, for Roman rule sat lightly on peaceful provinces such as this. For a typical Somerset village the six hundred years from, say A.D. 50 to A.D. 650 must have been at least as tranquil, with just a few exceptions, as the six hundred years from A.D. 1370 to A.D. 1970.

The next transition was much more dramatic and painful. Early in the ninth century the menace of the Vikings began to be felt. Now the ancient barriers which protected Somerset from events in 'mainland' Britain were useless. The new enemy came by sea and, moreover was already well established in Ireland.

Only fifty years after the West Saxon king Egbert rounded off his domain by the conquest of Devon and Cornwall, his grandson, Alfred, was a refugee on the Somerset marshland islet of Athelney, all that remained to him of his kingdom.

The story of Alfred's heroic recovery is recounted in Chapter 6. The peace he won lasted for over a hundred years (as far as Somerset, though not the rest of England, was concerned). It was broken in the reign of the unhappy Ethelred, known to history as The Unready, who had to fight a determined attempt by the Danish kings to annex his country. In the year 997 Danish hordes, landing in the west, did great damage in Somerset, and the sad story was repeated in 1003, when the Danish king himself, Sweyn, landed at Exeter and marched eastwards, ravaging the countryside as he went.

The first two decades of the eleventh century saw a succession of devastating incursions by the Northmen, and Somerset must indeed have been in an appalling plight. In 1016 the darkness was lifted a little by a battle won by the new king, Edmund, against Canute's army at Penselwood, but gloom descended again with the death of the young king a few months later.

The last English king, Harold, returning from exile in Ireland in 1052, landed at Porlock and made a triumphal progress eastwards. As we now know, the Norman Conquest loomed near. In 1067, the year after Hastings, the south-western shires rose in revolt but submitted to William the Conqueror after Exeter had endured a siege. For the long-suffering peasantry and merchants, the firm though stern Norman rule must have been an improvement rather than otherwise after the years of chaos.

From that time the ordeals of Somerset through foreign conquest were ended, though local warfare was, for a few more centuries, far too frequent. For instance, in 1087 there was much looting and murder in an abortive rising in favour of William's son Robert. Bath was burned, and Ilchester became the scene of a battle. Similar depredations were even more widespread during the lawless period of war when Stephen and Matilda were contending for the throne of England.

The county then settled down to a long period of relative peace —right until it was disturbed by the Civil War in the reign of Charles I. The towns grew, trade prospered, abbeys and monasteries were founded and played a dominant part in the life of the county. For the first part of the period much of the countryside was preserved in its primitive state, as hunting grounds for Norman and Plantagenet monarchs and so subject to the strict forest laws. The great forests of Somerset (and it must be remembered that 'forest' in this context did not necessarily mean an area covered by trees) were Exmoor, Selwood, Mendip, Neroche and North Petherton.

As the centuries passed, more and more of the former waste land, both hill moor and flooded levels, was claimed for agriculture, largely on the initiative of the great ecclesiastical landowners. In the fourteenth century immigrant Flemings introduced the technique of cloth-weaving to Somerset, and many of our towns, Taunton and Frome among them, became notable centres of the cloth trade. As the centuries passed, one after another of the Somerset towns obtained charters to hold fairs and markets. The ports developed their trade with Ireland, France and Spain.

Hostilities in the Civil War actually began in Somerset, with a skirmish at Street in August 1642. A battle was fought at Lansdowne, near Bath, in 1643. Much fighting occurred during the following year, and in October 1644 Parliamentarian forces were shut up in Taunton and closely besieged. They were rescued by an army under Fairfax in July 1645, Fairfax following up his success by defeating the Royalist general, Goring, in battles at Langport and Aller Moor. His troops soon afterwards occupied Bath, Bridgwater, Bristol and Wells, at which last place they did much damage to the cathedral. After this, the Royalists retreated to the West, their last foothold in Somerset being Dunster Castle, which surrendered in April 1646 after a siege of 160 days.

During these disturbances many of the countryfolk of Somerset and Dorset organized themselves into a society for mutual protection against the excesses of both armies. Known as the Clubmen, they were strong enough to engage in a battle with the Parliamentarian army, though they lost the fight (it was at Hambledon Hill, Dorset, in August 1645).

Forty years later, in 1685, Somerset was again the centre of the stage of English history for a few bloodstained months. Having landed at Lyme Regis, the Duke of Monmouth, illegitimate son of Charles II, was proclaimed king at Taunton on June 20th. His campaign was badly bungled and his intelligence services inefficient, for if he had marched boldly to London he could well have succeeded, as William of Orange did three years later. As it was, although he

1   *Cheddar Gorge*

gathered large numbers of ordinary citizens of Somerset, he got no nearer to London than Frome. Then, irresolute, he retreated to Bridgwater, engaged the loyal troops of James II on July 6th and was roundly defeated. The atrocities subsequently committed by the king's army, under Kirk, and the legal cruelties perpetrated by Judge Jeffreys make horrifying reading and were long remembered in Somerset.

In 1688 William of Orange, supported by a better army than the Duke of Monmouth ever had, passed through Somerset on his way to London. The only battle of the campaign, and it was no more than a skirmish, took place at Wincanton, after which William advanced unhindered to a capital vacated by a scared James II.

Thereafter no more armies in battle order marched along Somerset roads. At Wincanton the more violent aspects of the story of Somerset end. The emphasis for the next 300 years was on the peaceful development of industry in town and countryside, as will be unfolded in the following chapters.

2 *Nunney Castle*

2. Selwood and the East

Approaching Somerset from the east, as the traveller usually does, it is evident that here we have that rarity in England, a natural county boundary. It is not so much a line as a zone, a labyrinth of hills, streams and forests. The ancient grassy tracks, visible for miles across the ocean-like swell of the chalk downs of Wiltshire, plunge into the maze and are immediately lost.

This is the primeval Forest of Selwood, which once clothed the countryside in a mighty arc from the neighbourhood of Bath southwards into Dorset. It had width as well as length, extending well into Wiltshire around Warminster, where the woods of Longleat are its vestiges. The name 'Selwood', which is held to mean 'the Wood of Sallows', testifies to the waterlogged nature of the terrain in ancient times.

As in the greater part of England, the towns and villages of eastern Somerset are mainly of Saxon origin. They were evidently put on the ecclesiastical map by St Aldhelm, the first bishop of Sherborne, who died in the year A.D. 709. The events which led up to his activities in Selwood are as follows. *The Anglo-Saxon Chronicle* records for the year 658: 'In this year Cenwalh fought at Penselwood against the Welsh and drove them in flight as far as the Parret.'

Cenwalh was king of the West Saxons, and by this campaign he annexed all of eastern Somerset. He was succeeded, after the short reign of another king named Centwine, by Ina in 689. One of the greatest and most enlightened of the early Saxon kings, Ina was an enthusiastic Christian, eager to spread the faith.

Some years earlier an Irish missionary named Maelduib had founded a monastic colony in a northern corner of Selwood, in a forest clearing which is now Malmesbury. One of his scholars was Aldhelm, who seems to have been a near relation of the king. The entire kingdom of Wessex had hitherto comprised one bishopric, that of first Dorchester-on-Thames and later, when the see was re-moved, of Winchester. In the year 705 King Ina split this great diocese and established a see of Sherborne, to evangelize and organize the territory west of Selwood. Aldhelm was appointed its first bishop. In one of the earliest documents referring to his diocese it is actually called 'Selwoodshire', or, in the West Saxon tongue, 'Sealuudscire', and 'Sealuud' is exactly how a Somerset-man would pronounce the word today.

Aldhelm was 70 years old when he became bishop and he lived for only four more years. Like Pope John XXIII in our own time, however, he fitted a lot into those few years. Determined to in-vestigate his new diocese for himself, he took a sturdy ash-stick in his hand, threw a harp over his shoulder and set out on hiking ex-peditions. Up and down the length of Selwood he tramped. Memories long survived of how he would sit on a bridge playing his harp and singing songs of his own composition (a kind of early calypso) until a crowd of villagers gathered. Then he would preach the gospel and baptize any converts in the stream.

Church Bridge, in Bruton, is on the site of a bridge on which Aldhelm almost certainly stood and preached. Near by, on a slope well above flood level, he built Bruton's first church, on the site where the present parish church, dating from the fifteenth century, still stands. It seems, too, that near by he established a mission station, at a place called Holy Water Copse. It is near Godminster House. An adjacent field is known as Holy Fathers.

A few miles farther north Aldhelm preached on another bridge at Frome. Apparently he had been summoned there, presumably by a Christian sympathizer, for he timed his arrival to coincide with Mid-summer Eve, when the inhabitants were preparing for a boisterous pagan festival. To make matters worse, it seems to have been a Sunday. Taking his stand on the bridge, Aldhelm and the six monks who were with him, struck up a psalm. An audience having as-sembled, Aldhelm launched into his sermon, which apparently was strong on information about hell-fire.

He baptized a batch of converts there and then and left them to build Frome's first church. It was on the site of the present church (most of which is modern, though it has some Saxon and early mediaeval features,) which, interestingly, is dedicated to St John the Baptist. John the Baptist also, like Aldhelm, preached in the wilderness and baptized converts in the local river; and Midsummer Eve is, according to the Christian calendar, St John's Eve.

Frome church possesses a statue of St Aldhelm, holding the model of a church in his hand. In the town, too, is St Aldhelm's Boys' Home, built by the Church of England Waifs and Strays Society.

If we want to know what Aldhelm's churches looked like we shall have to go a short way over the Wiltshire border to Bradford-on-Avon. There the Saxon church of St Lawrence is of his foundation. None of his Somerset churches survives, but that at Doulting is dedicated to him, and, here again, he is commemorated by a statue; also by St Aldhelm's Well, which gushes out of the rock in what was formerly the vicarage garden. It is related that St Aldhelm once sat in the cold water while he recited the whole of a psalter, presumably as a salutary mortification of the flesh. In the Middle Ages pilgrims used to come to Doulting to bathe in this same spring.

It was here that Aldhelm died, in the year 709. He was taken ill while visiting a rich but pagan uncle named Kenred, whose name survives in the place-name, Cannard's Grave, a mile from Doulting and a well-known roadhouse nowadays for motorists travelling along the high road that follows the course of the Fosse Way. Feeling that his time had come, Aldhelm thought it inappropriate that a Christian bishop should die in the house of a heathen and instructed his attendants to carry him back to Doulting, where he died on a stone slab in the church.

That same day his spirit appeared to his friend, Bishop Eigwin of Worcester, requesting that his body be taken to his old home at Malmesbury. This was done in a pilgrimage which lasted seven days in early May, with a priest leading with a cross and monks following with tapers burning. People flocked to touch the bier and be healed of their infirmities.

The Bishop of Worcester ordered stone crosses to be erected at the seven resting places, and these survived for many centuries. Evidently the procession did not take the most direct route, which would have been along the Fosse Way, for Aldhelm crosses are known to have stood at Frome, Bath and Bradford-on-Avon. Part of the shaft of the Aldhelm cross at Frome is still to be seen in an interior wall of the tower of St John's Church. And a fragment of the Bath cross, which once stood by the Church of St Michael (now destroyed) by Bath Street, can be found in the choir vestry of Bath Abbey.

Who were these Selwood peasants among whom Aldhelm conducted his mission? That they lived in lowly huts is evident from
reference to wattle-and-daub, which was also the material of which
Aldhelm's first mission huts were made. Aldhelm was active in Selwood as early as 680, which is only just over 20 years after the campaign which added east Somerset to Wessex. The likelihood is, therefore, that many of the villagers were British, or Welsh, as the Saxons
called them. Somerset abounds in Celtic names, and on the western
fringe of Selwood, near Queen Camel, is a hamlet known as Wales.
Perhaps some of them were refugees, displaced by Kenwalh's victorious army. Or maybe Saxon settlers had been pushing deep into
the forest for many years before the conquest. Or, even more probably, the population of the forest was of mixed origin, descended, like
the population of much of Midland England, from outlaws, refugees
and drop-outs of both races. The king of the West Britons, whom
Kenwalh defeated, had a well-organized and civilized realm extending from Cornwall to the Forest of Selwood, but the forest itself must
have been a kind of no-man's-land, no doubt badly in need of missionary work.

Indeed, for over 100 years the Forest was a frontier zone. Fixed
chronological points are scarce in those confused centuries, but a key
date is 577, when the West Saxon king Ceawlin defeated a confedera-
tion of British kings, killing three of them, at the battle of Dyrham
(on the borders of Gloucestershire and Wiltshire). From 577 to 658,
when Kenwalh invaded Somerset, Selwood was certainly a boundary
between the two races.

It may have been so earlier. The fateful battle of Camlann, at
which the half-legendary Arthur, leader of the Britons, received his
mortal wound, is now usually placed in the year 538. Mount Badon,
the last of Arthur's twelve great victories, was probably fought 20
years earlier. Although the chalk-lands of Wiltshire are generally supposed to have been in British hands during that period (Sarum was
taken in 552), Cadbury Castle, if it were indeed the celebrated Camelot, is well back from any frontier that existed on the east side of
Wiltshire. Its natural role is to command the eastern gateway into
Somerset, south of Selwood.

With the aim of discovering whether it could indeed be linked
with traditions of Camelot and Arthur, Cadbury has been extensively
investigated in recent years. Though much work still remains to be

done on the material uncovered, an interim account of the excavations and of the story of Cadbury has been written in a splendid book
Cadbury/Camelot by Mr Leslie Alcock, director of excavations for
the Camelot Research Committee in the 1960s.

Men were camping on the hill in early Neolithic times. Pottery
has been tentatively dated 3600–3400 B.C.; a deer antler, around
2510 B.C. Occupation was desultory, however. There are no traces
of an early permanent settlement and certainly not of any fortifications.

Settled life on the hill-top evidently began in the late Bronze Age,
say in the eighth or seventh centuries B.C. At that time the climate
of southern England was becoming wetter and colder, so a tribe
which was living in the lowlands probably moved uphill to a dry
spot. The tribesmen apparently felt themselves to be in no danger
from human enemies, for they built no defensive walls.

The arrival of new tribes from the Continent, who understood the
art of smelting iron, marked the beginning of the Iron Age, and with
it a period of frequent wars. For the first time, probably in the sixth
century B.C., Cadbury was fortified. The first rampart was an ambitious undertaking. Says Mr Alcock:

'The circuit of the bank was a little over twelve hundred yards.
From this fact, something of the effort required to build Rampart A
may be calculated. About 900 stout poles would have been needed
for the front of the bank, together with a run of at least 70,000 feet
of planking for the shoring and the breastwork. The rear posts and
cross ties would have added yet more. So there was a major operation
involved in cutting and dressing the timber, before any defences
could be assembled. . . . It is quite evident that considerable communal effort and a strong organization were both involved.'

After an unknown period, this fort fell into grassy ruins for a
time, and then another, even more impressive, rampart was constructed. The foundations were dug down into solid rock, and the
rampart given a core of limestone slabs.

Successive occupations improved the defences until in the last
century before the Roman invasion (that is, in the first century B.C.
and the first century A.D.) Cadbury had grown into a sizeable town.
It was inhabited by people of the nation of Durotriges, who occupied
a large slice of territory in south-western Britain. Metal-workers,
potters, armourers, weavers, carpenters and many other craftsmen

were busily employed within the encircling fortifications of **Cadbury Castle**. There may even have been a mint, for bronze and silver Durotrigian coins have been found on the site; also iron bars used as currency.

After the landing of the Romans in Kent in A.D. 43, Vespasian, the Roman general who later became emperor, led the Second Legion on a campaign to subdue the West. In the course of it, so the historian Suetonius tells us, 'he fought 30 battles, conquered two warlike tribes and captured more than 20 *oppida*, as well as the Isle of Wight'. The two warlike tribes were the Durotriges and the Belgae, and the *oppida*, a word which means towns, were evidently the Celtic hill citadels. The outstanding example of a hill-top town in the West is, of course, Maiden Castle, the Celtic name of which was Dunum, which was the capital of the Durotriges. Excavations there have un-covered dramatic evidence of the storming of the town by the Romans. Skeletons in the emergency cemetery in which the slaugh-tered defenders were buried exhibit sword wounds, crushed skulls, the neat holes made by javelins, and, in one instance, a catapult bolt lodged in a vertebra.

One would have expected that Cadbury would certainly have to be included in the list of captured *oppida*, and, sure enough, evidence of its having been carried by storm has come to light. Inside the south-western gate is a mass grave testifying to a massacre of men, women and children. At the same time, the fortifications, including the gates, were as far as possible destroyed by fire.

Meticulous archaeological investigation, however, has shown the dangers of jumping to what seemed to be an obvious conclusion. The massacre did not occur in the 40s, at the time of Vespasian's cam-paign, but about 30 years later. Apparently the inhabitants of Cad-bury made peace with the Romans and continued to occupy their town for another generation.

History is completely silent about disturbances in southern Britain in the A.D. 70s. The Roman legions were busy up north, and the south was supposed to be peaceful and well on the way to becoming Romanized. Yet here was this massacre at Cadbury. Mr Alcock's interpretation is that the Romans decided to move the population from the hill-fort down to the lowlands and the Cadbury people, get-ting wind of what was happening, shut themselves in and resisted. An isolated episode, not worth the attention of any Roman historian, but tragedy for the inhabitants of Cadbury. The survivors dispersed to the neighbouring villages, notably South Cadbury (where much Roman pottery of the first and second century has been found), Queen Camel and Sutton Montis. The hill fort remained deserted for 400 years.

Roman civilization in Somerset was concentrated around the Fosse Way and around the branch road which led south from Ilchester through Yeovil to Dorchester. The section of the country which we are now considering lay east of that ruler-straight highway. Probably the farther one moved away from it, the less was Roman influence felt. In any case, the Roman era, after the initial phases, cannot be thought of as an alien occupation, for Britain enjoyed the same status as the other provinces which made up the Empire. Its regional government was controlled by local gentry, educated in Roman ways and saturated in Roman culture. Life among the lower classes probably continued much as ever it did.

One notable Romano-British site on Creech Hill, near Bruton, has proved on excavation to be a pagan temple. Coins, pottery and beads of the third and fourth centuries were found there, as well as several small bronze statues, of Minerva, Mars, Mercury and other gods. A Roman pavement is reputed to have been found at Discove, near Bruton, about 250 years ago; and about the same time a pig of lead, weighing about 50 lb and bearing an inscription indicating a date of about A.D. 164 was dug up. Whatley, near Frome, has the site of a Roman villa. At Shepton Mallet the excavation of the site of a Roman house revealed numerous coins covering almost the whole Roman period, from Claudius (A.D. 41) to A.D. 353. A Roman road led westwards across Selwood from Old Sarum to the mines on Mendip, and it was known that lead was being mined in Somerset as early as A.D. 49.

The civilization of four centuries was breached in the year 367, when in a concerted raid Picts, Irish and Saxons broke into Britain from all sides and killed and ravaged for more than a year. The Roman presence lingered for another 40 years, with armies crossing the English Channel, first in one direction (to support some British pretender to the Imperial throne) and then in the other (to rescue the unhappy province from new invaders). The last Roman intervention from the Continent probably occurred about the year 410, after which Britain was left entirely to its own devices.

For several decades the barbarian invaders had things more or less their own way, but resistance stiffened around the middle of the fifth century. Its leader was one Ambrosius, who seems to have emerged from the Cotswold villa society in what is now Gloucestershire. The sweeping onslaught of the Saxons from the east was checked, and visitors in the 480s found Britain a prosperous country. After Ambrosius the good work was carried on by that nebulous figure, Arthur—which brings us back to Cadbury Castle again.

In spite of frequent popular references to 'King' Arthur, Arthur was not a king. Just as the eastern part of Britain was in that age divided among a number of small Saxon kingdoms, so the western half was partitioned among at least five squabbling Celtic ones. We know the names of the kingdoms in Arthur's day and also the names of the kings. Our local Somerset monarch, king of Dumnonia, was Constantine, or Custennin, a treacherous character who, after disguising himself as an abbot and taking a vow of good behaviour, murdered two innocent young men in a church. Arthur himself was a military leader—the chronicles refer to him as *dux bellorum*—who apparently attracted a band of personal followers whom he welded into an irresistible fighting force. Alfred Duggan, in his historical novel about Arthur's adversary, Cerdic, suggests that Arthur's success was based on the re-introduction from the Continent of a supply of heavy horses. Hence the tales about King Arthur and his knights. It seems a logical idea. The Saxons were essentially foot-soldiers and would have little answer to a cavalry charge.

The legends and romances which have gathered around Arthur are, of course, later accretions. We shall notice some of them later when we come to Glastonbury. Arthur must, however, have been an outstanding character for the stories to attach themselves to him and to cling so long and stubbornly. If it were indeed the skeleton of Arthur that was exhumed at Glastonbury in the year 1191, he was a giant of a man, for Gerald of Wales, reporting the event, writes: 'The thigh bone, when placed next to the tallest man present, as the abbot showed us, and fastened to the ground by his foot, reached three inches above his knee.'

That so little is known about this splendid man is regrettable but understandable. Learning was one of the first casualties in the wreck of the Empire. The civilization of the Romans was replaced by an age in which even kings could not read or write. Events were recorded by only a few monks, writing in cells and cloisters, into which ruffians in search of loot or slaves might intrude at any time. Such records as were made stood a slim chance of survival in the turbulent centuries that followed, when the Anglo-Saxon invasion was succeeded by the even more terrible one of the Norsemen and Danes.

There is some indication, too, that Arthur was no great favourite of monkish chroniclers. A tough character, he seems to have been quite prepared to help himself to church property when the circumstances demanded it. Probably he received the same unsympathetic treatment as did Charles Martel who, although he saved France from the Saracen invasion, was sharply criticized by outraged churchmen whose property he requisitioned to help pay for the campaign. Gildas, a sour priest who was a contemporary of Arthur and who wrote a commentary on the age, could not even bring himself to mention Arthur by name, though his book, *De Excidio et Conquestu Britanniae* which bears the appropriate sub-title of *Liber Querulus* or *The Complaining Book*, hints of a shadowy background figure who was responsible for those 12 great battles in which the Saxons were thrown back across Britain.

The battles themselves are named, and much ingenuity has been expended in trying to identify them. Pet theories abound. The last article I wrote about Arthur and Camelot, tentatively identifying Camelot with Cadbury Castle, provoked a response from a reader who was sure that Arthur never set foot in Somerset in his life and that all the battles were fought in the lowlands of Scotland. Others have identified all the places, to their satisfaction, in the Midlands and North Wales, and even in the narrow limits of Sussex. The more widely held view nowadays, however, is that the battles covered a period of a number of years, during which Arthur and his troops ranged far and wide over Britain, fighting a campaign here in one year and far away on another salient in the next. There is a persistent tradition that Arthur was a West Countryman, and the story that he was born in Cornwall, made his headquarters at Camelot (Cadbury), fought his final battle against treacherous fellow Celts near by, and was interred at Glastonbury, is likely enough to be correct.

We shall come across tales of Arthur time and again as we explore other corners of Somerset, but Cadbury Castle is particularly rich in them. Within the ramparts is Arthur's Well, where Arthur's hounds drink deep on stormy nights in winter before following their master along the old bridle track known as Arthur's Hunting Path which leads towards Glastonbury. The horsemen are out again at all seasons when the moon is full. One can see the moonlight glinting on the horses' silver shoes. 400 years ago someone found a silver horseshoe at Cadbury.

The hill itself is hollow, according to local tradition. Any person pure in heart who went to Arthur's Well on Midsummer Eve and bathed his eyes in the water would see the hill open and, within it, Arthur and his knights sleeping their long sleep, their swords ready at hand, waiting for the call to awake when Britain is again in danger. In 1902 when an antiquary questioned neighbouring villagers about the site an old man asked anxiously, 'Are you come to take the king away?'

The little road which leads up to the Castle from South Cadbury church used to be known as Arthur's Lane. Not far away is a field called Westwoods which tradition says was where the battle of Camlann was fought; certainly some battle was, for numerous skeletons of men have been found in trenches there. If Arthur was carried, dying, to Glastonbury he would have crossed the bridge nowadays known as Pomparles, (the name is supposed to derive from *Pons Perilis*), where in a last supreme effort Arthur threw his sword, Excalibur, into the dark waters beneath.

The excavations conducted at Cadbury Castle in 1966–70 under the direction of Leslie Alcock were undertaken largely to test the possibility of there being a basis of truth behind these and similar traditions. It was too much to hope to find any direct reference to Arthur, but digging might well establish whether the site was occupied by an important chieftain at the appropriate date. In any event, the project ought to make a useful contribution to our knowledge of an obscure period.

So it proved. The excavations showed clearly that, after being abandoned for nearly 400 years, Cadbury Castle was re-occupied in the late fifth or early sixth centuries. Mighty new fortifications, mainly of timber, were constructed on top of the decayed Iron Age ramparts. The foundations of a massive gate tower were uncovered.

As the whole site occupies 18 acres, with a perimeter of 1,200 yards, only a small portion of the interior could be excavated. By a combination of inspired guessing and good luck, the excavators chose a sector which contained the foundations of an early sixth-century hall, impressive in size and construction. It was 63 feet long by 34 feet wide, with an open hearth in the centre. The obvious identification is that this was the feasting hall of a Dark Age chieftain. Mr Alcock suggests that a thousand men would be a reasonable size for the army of such a chieftain as Arthur might have been. 'And Cadbury itself,' he says, 'would be a suitable base for such a body.'

Must we say goodbye for ever to the Camelot of the romances? The many-towered castle, the 'silken-sail'd shallop skimming' along the river, the 'abbot on an ambling pad', 'the long-hair'd page in crimson clad' are all stuff of the twelfth century, as seen through the rose-coloured spectacles of Tennyson. Is it anything more?

I came across a hint that it was otherwise when reading Malory's *Morte d'Arthur* (he wrote in the fifteenth century). He recounts that after Sir Bedevere had watched the departure of the barge bearing Arthur's body to the Isle of Avalon, he went wandering in the forest.

'And in the morning he was sure, betwixt two holts hoar, of a chapel and a hermitage ... and when he came into the chapel he saw where lay a hermit grovelling on the floor, fast thereby was a new tomb graven. When the hermit saw Sir Bedevere he knew him well, for he was but little tofore Bishop of Canterbury....'

If we ask ourselves what the former Bishop of Canterbury was doing in the guise of a hermit in the West Country we shall conclude that the likeliest explanation is that he was a refugee. The Saxon invaders had chased him out of his diocese.

Shortly after reading this I was visiting Colchester, a sign at the entrance to which reminds us that it is 'the oldest recorded town in Britain'. The museum is filled with relics of Roman times. Before the Romans came Colchester was the capital of the British king Cunobelinus (or Cymbeline). Wrecked during the revolt of Queen Boudicca, it revived to become one of the most cultured, wealthy and sophisticated cities of Roman Britain. The museum (in the Norman castle which was erected on the site of the Roman civic temple) provides ample evidence of the luxury in which the citizens lived.

The end of Roman Colchester is silence. In an exposed and relatively indefensible position to invaders from across the North Sea, it must have fallen early to the Saxons. There is no reason to suppose that the pattern prevalent for other parts of the country (including Canterbury) did not apply here; that there were survivors who escaped westwards.

Far away in the refuge of an old hill-fort in the West Country, they would mourn for the lost glories of their old home. Nostalgically, they would call their sanctuary by the old familiar name, Camulodunum—Camulodun—Camelot. And recollections of the earlier Camelot, magnified and distorted by the mists of memory, might well have become the basis of the fair city immortalized by the mediaeval romances.

Before we leave Cadbury Castle we should note its final apearance in history. Neglected by the Saxons after their conquest of Somerset, it fell again into dereliction until early in the eleventh century. England was then again harried by invaders, this time the Danes, and the luckless Ethelred the Unready was on the throne.

On 13 November 1002 Ethelred ordered a general massacre of the many Danes who were living peaceably in England. The reaction of the formidable Danish king, Sweyn, was swift and predictable. He brought over a ruthless army and set about avenging his fellow-countrymen. Thereafter for a decade or so England was seldom free from marauding Danish armies. In August of the year 1009 a Danish leader named Thorkell the Tall arrived with the latest contingent and set about the task of devastation. He operated, say the chronicles, as far west as the Vale of Pewsey. Some time during that autumn or the following spring Ethelred re-occupied and re-fortified Cadbury Castle.

Mr Alcock's excavations revealed many traces of this period. One of the most interesting finds was a series of trenches, at first mysterious, which were later interpreted as being the foundations of a cruciform Saxon church which was never completed. There was a mint at Cadbury in this troubled time, the coins bearing the Saxon name of the hill-top town, Cadanbyrig. The moneyers who minted the coins had formerly operated from Ilchester. They were at Cadbury for only six or seven years. When peace returned to the land with the accession of Canute, a Danish king, they dispersed, mainly, it seems to Bruton and Crewkerne. Canute evidently caused the fortifications to be dismantled, and Cadbury disappears into oblivion. The excavators found that someone at some time had built another gate-house on top of the ruins of Ethelred's gate, but they concluded that it was intended to keep livestock in rather than enemies out.

Our preoccupation with Cadbury Castle has brought us across the borderline of historical times. The same century that saw the last refortification of Cadbury was also the century of the Domesday Book. Almost every village and manor in Somerset is in that catalogue.

Brief mentions in charters, grants and chronicles throw occasional gleams of light on Selwood manors in the intervening years. For instance, we learn that Bruton was a personal possession of King Ina about the year 690. In 955 King Edred died at Frome. The references, however, amount to little more than names and do not tell us much about the places or the people who lived there.

As more ambitious structures began to replace the flimsy wattle-and-daub of the villages which St Aldhelm evangelized, the inhabitants of eastern Somerset discovered a valuable asset in their building stone. One had only to dig to find an abundance of it. Doulting had a pleasant soft grey stone; Keinton Mandeville a hard but durable blue lias; while Ham Hill, farther west beyond Yeovil, produced a splendid golden stone which in time became celebrated all over southern England.

Among the first buildings to use local stone extensively in eastern Somerset were the Norman castles constructed in the years after 1066 to keep the restless countryside in order. None of the earlier ones now remains, but traces may be seen of the earthworks on which they once stood. Castle Cary, for example, takes its name from the Norman castle which once dominated it. The place was the stronghold of the Lovell family after the Conquest and was captured by storm by King Stephen in 1138. Penselwood has, as is appropriate to its strategic position, two castles, one known as Ballard's Castle or simply The Castle, the other as Castle Orchard, both skilfully sited. In the neighbourhood the Pen Pits, a collection of more or less circular depressions scattered over several hundreds of acres, have presented an enigma to generations of antiquaries. At one time popular conjecture identified them with the site of Pensauelcoit, a British city mentioned by Nennius in the ninth century, but now they are thought to have been quarries for building stone, probably used over a long period.

The earliest Norman castles were simple towers, or keeps, starkly designed for military use in a hostile land. Later they were expanded into much more elaborate and complex structures, with some consideration given to comfort and domestic convenience. The most imposing one surviving in eastern Somerset is Nunney Castle, which, although only a shell, still has most of its walls intact. Begun in 1373, it is a good example of a castle undergoing transition into a dwelling-house. While it has a strong cylindrical tower at each corner, the central part is occupied by a residential building originally of four storeys, the third of which consisted chiefly of a handsome domestic chapel. The end came for Nunney during the Civil War when, in 1645, a Parliamentary force well equipped with artillery bombarded it into surrender. To make restoration difficult if not impossible, the Roundheads tore out all the interior fittings, including joists and floorboards, and their policy proved so effective that the place was never subsequently inhabited.

Side by side with military edifices, the Normans built churches—austere, solid buildings with typical rounded arches. Few have survived in east Somerset. The general rule is that later ages have pulled down the old parish church and replaced it by another on the same site, though usually retaining the Norman font and in some instances the Norman tower and a few Norman doorways. Beckington is an example of a fine Norman church tower. Churches with Norman fonts are Lullington, which has a very fine one as well as several lovely Norman arches and pillars, Wheathill, West Camel, East Lydford, Weston Bampfylde, Templecombe and Charlton Horethorne.

Many of the plain Norman churches were demolished in the second great period of church-building, which was the late fifteenth and early sixteenth centuries. The accession of King Henry VII had finally brought to an end the internecine, bloody Wars of the Roses, in which the ancient nobility of England did its best to destroy itself, and had given peace to a weary land. At the same time, England was prospering commercially as never before, and the merchant class in particular was thriving. Comfortable manor houses were replacing the bleak castles, and the massive Norman churches yielded to lighter and more elegant buildings in the Perpendicular style. Fine work of this period may be seen in the churches of Buckland Dinham (the tower is fifteenth-century), Bruton (with a really magnificent tower, over 100 feet high), Batcombe (again with a splendid tower), Charlton Musgrove, Shepton Montague, Alford, Bebcary and South Barrow (both with fifteenth-century towers), Bratton Seymour, North Cheriton, North Cadbury, Cucklington, Milborne Port (with a fifteenth-century rood screen) and Evercreech.

Once the country had settled down after the Norman conquest, new abbeys and priories began to spring up, particularly in the wilder parts of England, where much land was still to be had without dislocating too many existing rights. Although tangled Selwood must have been, in some respects, such an area, the shadows of the great Abbeys of Glastonbury and Shaftesbury extended into its fastnesses and limited the scope of new enterprise.

However, several important ecclesiastical foundations were established. In 1142 a priory of Augustinian Canons was founded at Bruton. It was given a manor, the right to hold a market, and the charge of five local churches, namely, Wyke, Pitcombe, Redlynch, Shepton Montague and Brewham. The buildings were said to have been erected on the site of a Benedictine monastery which had stood there in early Saxon times, but no mention of such an establishment is made in the Domesday Book. The original strength of the community is said to have been 12 canons and a prior, which would be in keeping with that of similar foundations in other parts of the country. Throughout the Middle Ages the Priory added to its possessions, as testified by numerous grants and charters. In 1510 its status was raised to that of Abbey, and its first Abbot, Gilbert, undertook a vast improvement scheme at great expense. If he could have foreseen events he would probably have saved his cash, for in the reign of his successor, Abbot Ely, Henry VIII's axe descended and the Abbey was closed and sold. Bruton still has its Abbey Court-house, in its main street, a wall of the Abbey, and, high on a hill overlooking the town, the Abbey Dovecot.

On the Wiltshire border, beyond Penselwood, Stavordale Priory was another Augustinian establishment, founded in 1263. The church, built in the fifteenth century, survived the Dissolution and for many years served as a farm, the chancel being used as a dwelling-house and the nave as a barn. Early in the present century it was skilfully and imaginatively restored as a country house. It is privately owned.

Midway between Bruton and Frome lies Witham Friary, which had a religious establishment founded about the same time as Bruton Priory. The foundation is connected with the murder of St Thomas a'Becket. After Henry II had expressed contrition for the deed he was given as a penance by the Pope an obligation to undertake a three-years' Crusade to the Holy Land. Henry II, one of the most able

3   *Bath: the Roman Baths*

and forceful monarchs ever to occupy the English throne, naturally raised a strong objection to being absent for so long from his turbulent realm, so the Pope commuted the penance to the foundation of three Carthusian monasteries, the Carthusians being then unrepresented in England. Witham Friary was one of the sites chosen. Its third and greatest prior was St Hugh, who was afterwards bishop of Lincoln and died in 1200.

The parish church and the abbey dovecot are now all that remain of the Carthusian headquarters in England. It is thought that the church is the one in which the lay brothers of the Order worshipped.

The general prosperity of the later Middle Ages in eastern Somerset was not without its fluctuations, a reminder of which is the site of the abandoned village of Watcombe, near Corton Denham. Knolls, depressions and irregularities in the turf mark the foundations of a settlement the inhabitants of which probably perished of the Black Death in the mid-fourteenth century.

Henry VIII's spoliation of monasteries and abbeys from 1538 onwards was, naturally, marked by a scramble for shares in the loot. One of the lucky families in east Somerset was the Berkeleys. Sir Maurice Berkeley, who was then standard-bearer to the King, was given the Abbey and its lands at Bruton, where the family from that time forward made its home. We can see the tombs of members of the family in Bruton church. For his services to the Royalist cause during the Civil War, John Berkeley was after the Restoration created the first Baron Berkeley. He it was who invested part of his wealth in some acres of open country on the western edge of London and so gave the family name to Berkeley Square, while his home town is commemorated in Bruton Street near by.

The reigns of the later Tudors saw the establishment of many privately-owned schools in England, to fill the gap caused by the collapse of much of the educational work carried on by the church before the dissolution of monasteries. Chief benefactors, especially in the West Country, were rich merchants. Their fortunes were in general founded on wool. From the thirteenth century onwards numerous mills for weaving cloth, notably broadcloth, sprang up along the streams of eastern Somerset. A class of prosperous middlemen emerged, whose function was to buy the wool, pass it to small mills for spinning and weaving, and then transport it to London or Bristol for export. As Daniel Defoe, writing in the seventeenth cen-

4 *Bath: Lansdown Crescent*

tury, remarked of the wool merchants of Bradford, just over the border in Wiltshire:

'They told me at Bradford that it was no extraordinary thing to have clothiers in that county worth from £10,000 to £40,000 a man, and many of the great families who now pass for gentry in these counties have been originally raised from and built up by this truly noble manufacture.'

Defoe lists as the principal clothing towns of Somerset: Frome, Pensford, Phillips Norton, Bruton, Shepton Mallet, Castle Cary and Wincanton.

Both Bruton and Frome were early engaged in the trade. One of the first fulling mills in England was built on a stream near Bruton in 1290. And it is recorded that the father of John Henton, prior of Bruton from 1448 to 1498, was a cloth merchant, wealthy enough to give £400 towards the rebuilding of Bruton Church.

Another Bruton lad who made good was Hugh Sexey who, starting life as a stable boy, became an auditor to Queen Elizabeth I. He endowed a charity which was made responsible for the upkeep of a hospital or almshouse and which has for the past hundred years provided funds for the support of Sexey's Boys' School. The almshouse is a fine example of seventeenth-century domestic architecture. A little earlier, in the sixteenth century, King's School, Bruton, was founded by Edward VI.

Another effect of the dissolution of abbeys, monasteries and priories by the avaricious Henry VIII was the cessation of markets and fairs held under their auspices. Among them Stavordale market seems to have come to an end, so in 1556 we find the inhabitants of Wincanton obtaining a charter from Philip and Mary to hold a weekly market on Wednesdays as well as two annual fairs.

In the Civil War of the seventeenth century the little manufacturing towns of eastern Somerset were in general inclined to support the Parliamentary side, Puritan influence being strong. Most of the local gentry, on the other hand, were Royalist, including Colonel Frater, who surrendered Nunney Castle to a superior force of Roundheads. Armies of both sides passed through the area on several occasions, and King Charles I was at Bruton for a couple of nights in 1644, lodging at the Abbey, but no major battles were fought there.

Though Monmouth's Rebellion, which culminated in the Battle of Sedgemoor in 1685, was centred on Somerset, Monmouth's doomed

march towards Bristol, London and a crown took a route west and
north of the region we are now considering. After failing to find the
support he hoped for in Bristol, however, he retreated to Frome,
where he lost his resolution on receiving the news that the synchron-
ized rising of the Earl of Argyle in Scotland had also failed. His des-
pondency spread to his troops, 2,000 of whom are said to have
deserted while based on Frome. In due course revenge was exacted
on reputed rebel sympathizers in Frome, Wincanton and other
eastern towns by the terrible Judge Jeffreys. Twelve Frome men were
hanged, drawn and quartered, and their remains exhibited on village
greens, in market places and at cross-roads in the vicinity.

Thomas Ken, who was Bishop of Wells during this disturbed
period, is remembered in the West Country not only for his still-
popular hymns ('Awake, my soul, and with the sun' and 'Glory to
Thee, my God, this night') and for his resolute defiance of two kings
for the sake of his conscience but also for his kindness and compas-
sion. He courageously though vainly interceded for the victims of
Judge Jeffreys' peregrination of vengeance. Dying in 1711, he is
buried at Frome, 'under the east window of the chancel, just at sun-
rising', as he had requested.

Thereafter the story of eastern Somerset has been one of unevent-
ful peace. Typical of the placid eighteenth and nineteenth centuries is
Parson Woodforde, whose distinction lies in literature rather than in
war. The son of a rector of Ansford, close by Castle Cary, he first
served as curate to his father there and then, in 1764, became curate
of Babcary. His diaries are filled with homely details about his pur-
chases of cider, his games of fives against the church wall, his lost
wagers, the couples he married and the epicurean meals he enjoyed.

The towns of eastern Somerset and some of the larger villages are
composed mostly of houses of eighteenth and nineteenth century
construction, with modern bungalow estates and groups of council
houses as only partially absorbed annexes. The paucity of older
buildings in at least some of them is explained by the frequency of
devastating fires in earlier centuries—not surprising in view of the
ubiquitous thatch of those days. Wincanton, for instance, has records
of a disastrous conflagration in 1707, when the total loss exceeded
£3,000, a substantial sum for the early eighteenth century. Many of
the attractive stone houses and inns that now characterize Wincanton are the work of a local architect, Nathaniel Ireson, of that time.

Much of the older architecture of eastern Somerset, as of else-where, was, of course, demolished to make way for the building pro-grammes of the Victorians. In parish after parish we find records of the church having been 'restored' in the 1870s and 1880s. With the Norman and early Tudor eras, this was one of the three great ages of church building in the West Country, though the Victorians tended to imitate older styles rather than evolve anything new.

Frome is now the largest of the east Somerset towns, still with flourishing cloth mills and a number of other factories. Evercreech has, under the shadow of its magnificent church tower, factories for cheese processing and the making of soft drinks and fruit squashes. Twine is manufactured at Castle Cary. Wincanton has, besides its milk factory, the needs of travellers on the crowded A303 road to keep it busy. In general, however, the little towns thrive as shopping centres for the surrounding villages. In the villages themselves, agri-culture still predominates, with dairying as a speciality, though more and more of the cottages are occupied by families who travel con-siderable distances, such as to Yeovil or Bath, to their daily work.

3. Bath and the Avon Valley

Like an old cottage in a village overtaken by suburban development, Bath is in Somerset but not on the same terms as most other Somerset towns. It was there long before any county of Somerset existed. Its recent transference to the new county of Avon seems appropriate enough, for to the Avon valley it belongs, and the Avon, though a convenient northern boundary for Somerset, has an entity of its own.

Farther north the Cotswolds, an oblique barrier across England, guide the river Severn into the Severn Sea. Having performed this task, they huddle in a chaos of tumbled hills and deep valleys at the southern end of the county of Gloucestershire and spill over into Somerset to join up with the Mendips and Selwood. The Bristol Avon, having collected waters from most of the meadows of northern Wiltshire, plunges determinedly into their rocky confusion and forces its way, through clefts and gorges, westwards to the sea. Midway along this Titan's track the city of Bath has grown.

Once in a remote district of Zambia I chanced upon a warm spring bubbling from the earth and wriggling away through vividly green meadows much like the hot springs of Bath must have done in primeval times, before men discovered and exploited them. The tribe which lived near by had little use for it, except for washing clothes. So must the British tribe that roamed the Cotswolds three or four millennia ago have regarded Bath's mineral springs, though perhaps they found the warm waters convenient and pleasant in winter.

Concerning the discovery of the curative properties of the waters a fine old legend has survived. It was recounted by an early romancer, the mediaeval Geoffrey of Monmouth, as follows.

In the eighth century B.C. a king, Hudibras, ruled over a kingdom which reached from Cornwall to the Cotswolds. He had a clever son named Bladud, who contracted leprosy (a term which covered almost any skin complaint). In accordance with the hygenic rules of those times, Bladud had to be banished from human society. His sorrowing mother gave him a ring to take with him. Away he went, an outcast.

Where the king's court was is not recorded, but Bladud seems to have had some extensive wanderings before he found himself by the Avon, near Keynsham, where he got a job as a swineherd. (We are reminded of the story of the Prodigal Son.) It was not long before the pigs caught leprosy from him. On discovering this, Bladud took his herd foraging in the woods well away from his master's domain, while he pondered what to do to avoid being sent on his journeying again. He camped at what is now Swainswick ('Swine's-wick', according to one derivation), from where the pigs used to scamper down to the riverside to wallow in the hot springs.

He noticed that the change of scene was doing the pigs good but did not connect this with the hot springs until one day he lost a prime sow. When he discovered her again several days later she was wallowing in black, warm, oozy mud and had lost all symptoms of leprosy. Bladud then got the message and tried the mineral springs for himself. Every day for a week or two he enjoyed a hot mud bath, and gradually the leprosy healed.

His master, when Bladud and the pigs arrived back at Keynsham, at first refused to believe the crazy tale. Eventually he was persuaded, against his better judgment, to go with Bladud to the king's court where, after some initial misunderstandings, the prince identified himself by his mother's ring. In due course he succeeded his father to the throne, and during his reign he built a new capital city—where else but at Bath? It was called Caer Badon, the city of baths; or, according to other versions, Caer Yrn Naint Twymin (the city of the warm valley) or Caer Ennaint (the city of anointing).

Bladud is still remembered at Bath, where there are two statues of him, one at King's Bath and the other at Cross Bath. He also featured in the 'Thousand Years of Monarchy' celebrations held in the city in 1973. But whether he ever existed is, of course, open to doubt, though the story of the pigs seems quite a possibility.

Anyway, it seems likely that there was a settlement at or near Bath before the Roman invasion. When the Romans dedicated their baths there to the goddess Minerva they found she had to share the tutelage with a British goddess, Sul, who had prior rights. So the goddess, by a typical Roman compromise, became Sul-Minerva. And Bath was known as Aquae Sulis—the waters of Sul.

In accordance with Iron Age practice, the Celtic town of those times would probably be within the ramparts of a hill fort. The obvious place would be Soulsbury Hill. Down by the river, where the hot springs bubbled, there might well have been a grove and a shrine where offerings were made to Sul.

Whatever existed, the Romans soon made alterations. The insubstantial buildings in their setting of trees were replaced by massive palaces of the local white oolitic stone, which weathers to a soft golden tint. The ancient mud wallow was enlarged and excavated to form a pool, and the pool lined with lead to form a bath. Then more baths were added. The main one was encased in a bath-house, and just across the road or square a stone temple and a building that was probably a theatre were erected.

Of the town which grew up around the baths we know little, except that its wall (earthen with perhaps a superstructure of stone) followed much the same line as that of mediaeval Bath. It enclosed an area of 23 acres. Probably its population was about equal to that of mediaeval Bath, which is known to have been 1,500. However, as Roman Bath endured for more than 400 years, no doubt there were fluctuations.

The reason for our incomplete knowledge is that successive cities have been superimposed on the Roman foundations. The eighteenth-century renaissance made a fairly clean sweep of the mediaeval city, just as the mediaeval builders doubtless demolished the Saxon town and the Saxons used stone from the Roman ruins to build their own houses. The statement that Bath rests on hollow foundations is accurate. Beneath the street levels exists a labyrinth of cellars. The Roman remains are from ten to 15 feet below the present ground surface. Professor Barry Cunliffe has indulged in the splendid dream of supporting the whole of the modern city on pillars and laying bare beneath it, in crypts which would be a tourist paradise, everything that remains of the Roman era. Regrettably, it is likely to remain a dream.

Even the little we can see at present is impressive. The visitor, paying his admission fee at the entrance just across the stone-flagged precinct from the Abbey and descending to the Roman level, is surprised at the extent of what remains. It is like entering one of the dramatic caves beneath the Mendips or like rolling back, with a magic sesame, the door to a strange and hidden world.

The great central bath, 80 feet long, was probably open to the sky, as it is now, but around were cloisters with benches and recesses for statues and memorial tablets. The great bath was for swimming and total immersion, but in antechambers were the usual Roman facilities for hot and cold plunges—the *caldaria* and *tepidaria*. We can see the pillars on which the floors of these rooms were raised, to be heated by the standard Roman system (unhappily abandoned for so long), the hypocausts. We can still see the iron-tinged water pouring along the channels by which the Romans guided it, may still sit on Roman masonry and dabble our fingers in the steaming flood, which is just the right heat for the skin to bear comfortably. The Corinthian columns, the stone steps down to the pool, the general air of reasonably good repair that pervades the whole Roman complex, make it difficult to realize that 15 centuries have passed since Roman figures in togas came striding in to enjoy the waters and to gossip with their friends. We wonder whether it is worth while to wait till after lunch, in case they come back.

As visitors we are well catered for, the various features of the baths being adequately identified and described by discreet plaques. The attached museum rooms are rich in Roman remains, from coffins and moulded masonry to brooches, tools and coins.

It is a mistake to suppose that the bathers who came to Bath to enjoy a holiday or cure their ailments or offer their respects to Sul-Minerva were Mediterranean folk, glad to find a warm place in this cold country to which they were exiled. The Roman Empire was cosmopolitan. You could meet a Briton in Syria or Morocco or an Armenian or Egyptian in Britain. Most of the local people, however, would be born and bred locally, and the gentry who came visiting to Bath would be mostly Celtic aristocrats who had had a Roman education and training.

So when the Roman armies melted away, the Roman inhabitants of Britain did not 'go home'. They were at home already. They simply carried on their normal life, as far as possible, without the legions to protect them. Which explains why, although the last Roman cohorts are supposed to have crossed the Channel in about the year 410, a hundred years later Bath was still functioning as a spa for the local Romano-British population.

One popular theory suggests that Bath was the Mount Badon, where Arthur won the last of his 12 great battles against the Saxons. It seems likely enough. At any rate, in the time of Arthur, Bath was firmly in British hands. It was not until the year 577 that the West Saxon king Ceawlin, defeating the Celts in a battle at Deorham (Dyrham, on the borders of Wiltshire and Gloucestershire), broke through to the Severn Sea and split off the British kingdoms of the south-west from those in Wales. Bath was among the spoils that the Saxons collected by this campaign.

As with their other conquests of old Roman cities, they had little idea of what to do with it. The Saxons were not great builders. They regarded big stone buildings with doubt and dread, the haunt of the spirits of the great men and giants who had built them in an unreal past. So Bath, the white city in its deep valley, mouldered and collapsed into ruin.

Bath possessed, however, one asset, other than its mineral springs, which ensured that it would not be entirely abandoned and forgotten. It was situated on the Fosse Way, that strategic Roman highway which transects England from Lincoln to the south coast near Seaton. The Saxons were as poor at road-building as at the construction of stone houses—the rivers were their highways—so for more than 1,000 years after Britain became England the Roman roads continued to be the country's major land arteries. The section of the Fosse between Bath and Cirencester was known to the Saxons as Akeman Street, and Akemanceaster was one of their names for Bath.

An early charter of about A.D. 676 records the grant of land near Bath to the Abbess Bertana, as an endowment for a nunnery which evidently had been recently founded or was about to be founded. St Aldhelm built a little church, dedicated to St Michael, by the hot springs. And between 750 and 760 another church, dedicated to St Peter, was probably built. So we get a picture of a little town gradually developing around ecclesiastical establishments, as so many Saxon towns did.

By the year 973 Bath was sufficiently important to be chosen for the coronation of a king of all England, Edgar. Probably the choice was dictated by St Dunstan, Archbishop of Canterbury, who was himself a Somerset man and was the power behind the throne. Under Dunstan's régime, the Abbey, into which the seventh-century nunnery had developed, had been transferred to the Benedictine Order and was evidently flourishing. The *Anglo-Saxon Chronicle* speaks of 'a great congregation of priests and goodly company of monks and wise men gathered together' for the coronation.

The thousandth anniversary of this event was celebrated with much pageantry in Bath in 1973. In devising the coronation ritual and ceremony Dunstan was starting more or less from scratch, for there had never been anything quite like it before. He made such a good job of it that it still remains the basis of the coronation service used today.

The citizens of Bath were so pleased with the honour that from that time onwards they held an annual celebration at Whitsuntide, when they elected a 'King of Bath' for the ensuing year. One such 'king', elected in the eighteenth century, was Beau Nash.

A young man who probably witnessed the coronation was Aelfeah, or Alphege, who was born in the village of Weston, near Bath, in 953. In 975 he became Abbot of Bath and has been at times credited with the foundation of the Abbey, though probably he added to and improved buildings already in existence. Aelfeah it was who later became Archbishop of Canterbury and was martyred by the Danes at Greenwich in 1012. Incensed by his refusal to collect a huge ransom from his flock, and, being well primed with ale and mead, they pelted him with ox bones till he died. He is commemorated in a London church.

It was in that same year, 1012, that Bath makes one of its infrequent apearances in Saxon history, for Sweyn, king of Denmark, arriving in England on a mission of vengeance for all the Danes slaughtered in a recent massacre, made for a time his headquarters at Bath and there received the submission of the local lords and landowners.

In the reign of Edward the Confessor an event occurred which had an important influence on affairs in Bath throughout the Middle Ages. The king married Edith, a daughter of the Earl of Wessex, who was lady of the manor (to use a term which was not invented till later!) of that part of Bath which did not belong to the Abbey. Later the virtually celibate Edward packed her off to a nunnery but was sufficiently worldly-wise to retain all her property for himself. Bath thus became split between royal and ecclesiastical landlords, and so it remained for centuries, with predictable intermittent friction.

The Normans, who unlike the Saxons were mighty builders, naturally took Bath in hand. John of Tours, who was made bishop of Wells by William II (Rufus) in 1088, moved the seat of his diocese to Bath and set about replacing the old Abbey by an imposing new cathedral. Fragments of his building still remain in the present Abbey—the cloisters, for instance, and an arch at the east end of the south aisle in the chancel. Bishop John also took an interest in the hot springs. In addition to restoring three principal baths he built two more, one of them for public use. A twelfth-century writer mentions that 'sick persons from all over England go there to bathe in the healing waters, as well as the healthy, who go to see the wonderful outpourings of water and bathe in them'.

Although the baths continued to be used throughout the Middle Ages, little is recorded about them. Local history tends to centre around disputes between the Bishop of Bath and Wells and the exceedingly powerful Abbot of Glastonbury, who held vast estates in the West Country and of whom we read in Chapter 5. At one time, towards the end of the twelfth century, a Bishop of Bath and Wells, Savaric, successfully intrigued to get himself appointed Abbot of Glastonbury, regardless of the rights of an existing Abbot. He styled himself Bishop of Bath and Glastonbury. His income must have been enormous. However, his successor was prevailed upon to return to the old arrangement, and Glastonbury again became an independent abbacy.

Early in the sixteenth century, under the bishopric of Oliver King, the old Norman church, which had been neglected, was pulled down and a magnificent new edifice in the Perpendicular style erected. It was the last large church in this light, airy, elegant style to be built before Henry VIII dissolved the monastic establishments, and is a supreme example of Perpendicular architecture. Probably because the Bishop realized that the revenues of the see were inadequate, the new Abbey church was considerably smaller than its predecessor, built partly on the same foundations but occupying little more than the space of the Norman nave. It remains substantially as it was built, though with a Jacobean timber roof to the nave and though a good deal of restoration work was carried out in Victorian times. Its architects were William and Robert Vertue, masons employed by King Henry VII. William was a master of the art of vaulted masonry, and his chancel vaults at Bath Abbey are among the outstanding glories of English architecture. Walking through the Abbey is like strolling through a woodland glade, with sunbeams filtering through the tracery of tree branches on every side. The pillars which support the roof do not obtrude; their massive strength tapers off into delicate carving and foliations, much as tree trunks merge into branches, twigs and leaves. On a summer day the whole building, when viewed from within, seems to be afloat in a pool of light.

Meantime, the town outside was flourishing and growing. At various times during the Middle Ages charters for fairs and markets were granted, though all have now been discontinued. Before most other Somerset towns, Bath developed a woollen industry. Chaucer's Wife of Bath, in the *Canterbury Tales*, had an interest in cloth-making. The industry seems, however, to have been in decline by Tudor times.

With the Dissolution of Monasteries the old division of the city between Abbey and townspeople (who had succeeded to the King's share) was at an end. Thenceforth the city Corporation was dominant. One of the first effects of the change was, unhappily, the despoiling of the Abbey church. The city having for certain involved and rather obscure reasons declined to buy the church for 500 marks, the building was robbed of its lead, glass, bells and almost everything else removable and was then sold privately. This was in 1539, and it was not until 1572 that the city acquired the shell of the church, as a gift. As mentioned earlier, the nave roof is Jacobean, added by Bishop Montagu (1618–76) in direct consequence, it is said, of the bishop getting thoroughly soaked when trying to shelter from a rain-storm in the unroofed church.

The baths, which had been church property, also passed to the Corporation, who appointed a Keeper of the Baths. The Keeper, in fact, paid for the privilege and presumably derived his income from charges to clients or from tips. By 1673 the post had been commercialized to the extent that the water was being bottled and sent, for medicinal use, to towns all over the West of England and to London. A new bath was constructed, for the exclusive use of women, in 1576. It was known as the Queen's Bath after it had been used by Queen Anne, wife of James I, in 1613, and was demolished in Victoria's reign to expose the Roman bath which had been discovered directly beneath it.

In the early campaigns of the Civil War of the seventeenth century an important battle was fought on Lansdown Hill, overlooking Bath. It can be reckoned a drawn match, for while the Royalist army was left in occupation of the hill, after an heroic fight by both sides, the Parliamentarians continued to hold Bath, the prize for which the battle had really been fought. However, within a few weeks (this happened in the summer of 1643) the Royalists were back again and this time they entered Bath and stayed in control for two years. The city surrendered to the Parliamentarian general Fairfax in July 1645.

Evidently the ordinary citizens of the city suffered considerably during these disturbances, for the Mayor, in a letter, revealed: 'Our houses are emptied of all useful furniture, and much broken and disfigured; our poor suffer for want of victuals, and rich we have none. I dare not send a man on horseback, as the horse would be taken.'

Bath had had enough of wars and revolutions, and when in 1685 the Duke of Monmouth sent a deputation inviting support they threw the envoys out and shot one of the escort. However, they were wise enough to support King William III when he landed three years later.

Thereafter the history of Bath seems to be that of a procession of visitors to the baths. Most of the kings and queens in turn made the pilgrimage along the Bath Road, and among the earlier patrons were Samuel Pepys and Celia Fiennes. Pepys found the baths 'pleasant, and the manner pretty enough, only methinks it cannot be clean to go so many bodies together in the same water'. However, Celia Fiennes records that the baths were emptied and refilled twice a day. They were managed with considerable decorum, with a strict 'serjeant' in charge. Ladies had female attendants and for bathing wore a yellow canvas gown. When they emerged, dripping, from the baths, someone threw a flannel garment over their heads and stripped off their wet costume underneath. The ladies were then placed in enclosed chairs and carried off to their bedrooms.

Pepys refers to the excellent music he heard at Bath, but there was no general programme of concerts or indoor events, nor, indeed, anywhere suitable for them to be held. Bath had, however, tennis courts and bowling greens and pleasant walks under trees by the river.

From our survey of the fortunes of Bath to this date, it is obvious that the development of the city into a spa and centre of society was no sudden metamorphosis. Apart perhaps from an hiatus in

Saxon times, there was no real break in continuity between the fifth and the eighteenth centuries. Always there were visitors bathing in the waters, or drinking them. A succession of authorities, ecclesiastical in the Middle Ages, secular thereafter, made sundry provisions for catering for them.

Into this already lively scene there intruded, in 1705, a gentleman of fortune, Richard Nash, then aged 31. His father, a glass manufacturer of Swansea, had sent him to Oxford, bought him a commission in the Guards and made sundry other attempts to get him to settle down to a sober, industrious life. Richard, an extrovert and exhibitionist, preferred something easier and more exciting. He chose to spend his time with society women and splendidly dressed men, whom he strove to surpass in sartorial splendour. The wherewithal apparently came chiefly from gambling, though a colleague once remarked to him: 'I don't wonder at your losing money, but all the world is surprised where you get it to lose.'

Gambling was, in fact, the foundation on which the eighteenth-century prosperity of Bath was built. Enormous fortunes were being amassed by landed gentry, which included many new-rich who had made their money in industry and overseas ventures and were now investing it in land. Taking the waters was a good excuse for their coming to Bath, but when they were there they wanted facilities for other activities than bathing. And gambling was the rage.

A year or so before Richard Nash's arrival the Bath Corporation, in an attempt to impose some sort of order and organization into the dangerous chaos that was developing, appointed a Master of Ceremonies, Captain Webster. He had little idea what was expected of him and was before long killed in a duel. He held office long enough, however, to instal Nash in a post as gentleman-in-waiting—whatever that might involve. And, on Webster's death, Nash succeeded him as Master of Ceremonies—unpaid.

Thereafter for about 50 years he more or less ran Bath. As we have already noted, he was once elected the traditional 'King of Bath'. He set standards of behaviour and dress and exercised an autocratic control over the social life of the city. The habituées apparently loved it. 'I reign here,' he once told a princess, 'and my laws must be kept.' Nevertheless, he was a kind-hearted man, and his rule was on the whole beneficent.

Gambling, apart from on horses and dogs, is primarily an indoor occupation, and Bath lacked adequate accommodation for the crowds who wished to indulge. One of Nash's first acts, therefore, was to cause the Old Pump Room to be erected. Two theatres and a cold bath room followed, and then a fine Assembly Room with, a little later, a ballroom.

In collaboration with Beau Nash, three factors now contributed to the emergence of Georgian Bath. One was the development of stone quarries on Claverton Down by a Cornish merchant, Ralph Allen. The second was the opening of a navigable waterway, incorporating the Avon, from Bristol to Bath, thus allowing soft timber to be brought inland from the port. The third was the arrival in Bath of an imaginative builder and architect, John Wood.

This was the beginning of the age of great country houses in the Palladian style, in the building of which Wood had had some experience. An amateur antiquarian, he had filled himself with a plethora of nonsense about ancient Britain and its history (he was responsible for the perpetuation of the story of Bladud and Hudibras, mentioned earlier in this chapter), and he had the idea of restoring Bath to its classical splendour—a snow-white city of majestic buildings as he imagined it was in Roman times. He did not apparently prepare a comprehensive plan for the whole city but worked at various projects piecemeal, as opportunity offered.

Between 1724 and 1754, when he died at the early age of 49, Wood succeeded in reconstructing large sections of the city. His work was continued by his son, John Wood the younger. By the time he too died, in 1775, the miracle had been completed, and Bath stood, a stone city far more splendid than anything the Romans ever devised. Much of it survives to this day as its Georgian architects left it. Its terraces, its magnificent crescents, its perfectly proportioned town houses, are mostly the work of the two Woods. For Ralph Allen they designed the lovely villa in Prior Park, now a Roman Catholic school. Their work was continued by Robert Adam, who built the exquisite Pulteney Bridge, with its row of small shops.

One needs at least a week to discover and appreciate the treasures of Georgian Bath. Everywhere are spacious streets, secluded squares, fine wrought-ironwork, elegant bridges, exquisitely decorated interior walls and ceilings, classic fireplaces, graceful columns, bow windows and other architectural features characteristic of the period. We may spend an interesting day seeking out the memorial plaques to the celebrities who visited the city—Oliver Goldsmith, Jane Austen, Mrs Sarah Siddons, Gainsborough, Haydn, Macaulay, Thackeray, Fielding, Dr. Johnson, Sheridan, and numerous aristocrats and royals. Weary, we may sit in Regency chairs in the Pump Room and sip coffee while we watch tourists pulling wry faces as they sample the healthful but vile-tasting waters.

After all the eighteenth-century activity Bath in the next century went into a minor eclipse. It expanded in size and population, and much money was spent on improving the amenities, but fickle fashion had temporarily deserted it. Which was a serious deprivation for Bath, a city which had come to rely largely on the wealth brought in by visitors.

However, it persevered with all the general 'improvements' of the century. Gas-lighting was introduced; then in 1840 the Great Western Railway linked it with London. A city water supply was installed in 1851; a sewage system in 1866. Much new building took place, particularly of schools, hospitals and hotels, as well as a library and art gallery, but fortunately without depriving the city of much of its Georgian heritage. Several industries opened new factories.

The present century has brought its share of problems to Bath. Traffic congestion is intense, particularly as the city, set in a deep, narrow valley, has little elbow room. New building development has, however, climbed the slopes of the encircling hills, and Bath has become an important industrial city with a working population of nearly 50,000 and a total population of nearly double that number. It is easily the largest town in Somerset—or was until it was transferred to the new county of Avon. It has a modern university and also houses the Admiralty, now operating under an alias, the Department of Defence (Navy).

Tourism, however, remains its best money-spinner. In summer the city is crowded with visitors of all nationalities, attracted not only by its reputation but by the fact that so much can be seen in such a small compass. One strolls from modern department stores (and Bath is an excellent shopping centre) into Bath Abbey, roughly contemporary with the discovery of America, and thence, across a stone-paved square and down some flights of steps, into fourth-century Roman Britain. The waters may still be partaken of by those with faith in their medicinal properties (or with a healthy sense of curiosity). It is still possible to sit where Regency beaux and belles sat,

5 *Bench end, East Brent (Top left); Bench end, Bishops Lydeard (Top right); Font, Banwell (Bottom left); Pulpit, Trull (Bottom right)*

in the Pump Room. The fine old Georgian houses still fulfil utilitarian purposes as homes, offices and shops.

Bath also aspires to build up a reputation as a patron of the arts. It is not a new ambition. Starting with an impressive pageant in 1909, the idea of an arts festival has been revived time and again, the latest occasion being the ambitious 'Thousand Years of Monarchy' which provided a programme throughout much of the summer of 1973. Most of the necessary ingredients, except perhaps an adequate Arts Centre, are there.

Over in Wiltshire, especially in the chalk country, the villages tend to cower on the valley floors, but here in the Avon valley they camp upon the hilltops as well as by the river and its tributaries. How many of the hill sites are identical with those occupied in Romano-British times we cannot say. Certainly the narrowness of the valley would limit the number of villages that could find space in it, but the whole area suggests a bewildering medley of races. The name of Englishcombe, 'the valley of the English', for instance, suggests that there were other valleys near by occupied by Welsh, or Romano-British. The countryside is studded with Roman villas (as at Camerton, which has at least three, Langridge, Monkton Combe, Newton St Loe and Farleigh Hungerford). In addition to Solsbury Hill there are several hilltop earthworks, occupied in Iron Age times, as at Duncorn Hill, near Dunkerton, Pendown, near Priston, and Barrow Hill, near Englishcombe. There is also that enigmatic earthwork, the Wansdyke, which extends right across Wiltshire and half-encircles Bath on the southern side. From the fact that it cuts across Roman roads and other evidence it is held to belong to the Dark Ages, probably the sixth century A.D., and it is constructed as a defence against an enemy from the north. Now which nation was north of the Wansdyke in the sixth century—the Romano-British or the Saxons? The Saxons are generally supposed to have been, which puts Bath in Saxon territory at a pretty early date.

The hills support monuments to later ages. Lansdown Hill has one, erected in 1720, to the men who fell at the Battle of Lansdown in 1643, and another, the Lansdown Tower or Beckford's Folly, erected by that eccentric genius William Beckford, in 1825. Beckford had a brilliant brain spoilt by lack of discipline, he having inherited a vast

6   *Wells Cathedral*

fortune from sugar estates in the West Indies. His architectural extravagances included, besides his folly on Lansdown Hill, a precarious tower to a great mansion at Fonthill, in south Wiltshire, from which he could see the Lansdown tower nearly twenty miles away.

On Claverton Hill, on the other side of Bath, Claverton Manor, which was built in 1819, now houses the American Museum : an unexpected feature, this, to find in the Somerset countryside. The finely-proportioned rooms hold meticulous reconstructions of domestic interiors in pioneering America in the seventeenth, eighteenth and nineteenth centuries, as well as many splendid examples of craftwork. The Museum is justifiably much visited during the summer, from April to November, and by no means exclusively by American tourists.

Ignoring Limpley Stoke, which occupies an intruding salient of Wiltshire, the next two villages up the valley from Claverton are Freshford and Farleigh Hungerford, particularly beautiful in their wooded riparian setting. Both, indeed, belong to the valley of the little river Frome, which joins the Avon at Freshford, the Avon itself swerving eastwards there. Farleigh Hungerford is dominated by its castle, now in ruins, which for over 300 years, from 1369, was the home of the Hungerford family. Sir Thomas Hungerford, who died in 1396, was the first Speaker of the House of Commons. Although the Hungerford family suffered considerably when the old aristocracy were busily exterminating each other in the Wars of the Roses, the line survived down to the time of the Civil War, when two Hungerfords appeared on opposite sides. The castle endured a short siege but was not demolished as were so many other West Country castles. The Sir Edward Hungerford who held the estates after the Restoration did his family more harm, however, than any wars in which they had engaged, for he squandered the entire family fortune, had to sell the estates and castle (which was subsequently allowed to fall into ruins) and died in poverty. The great keeps of the castle are now shells, and the only feature surviving intact is the family chapel, now used as a museum.

A mile or two up a deep-cleft tributary valley from Farleigh is Hinton Charterhouse, which derives its name from the Carthusian priory which was founded here in 1232, by Ela, Countess of Salisbury. Much of the priory remains and has been tastefully restored. We can see the chapterhouse, undercroft, dovecots and parts of the guest house, while the fifteenth- or sixteenth-century gatehouse has been incorporated in a dwelling-house.

Just over the hills lies Norton St Philip, which we have already mentioned in Chapter 2 (for we are now on the borders of Selwood). Here is a lovely mediaeval hostelry, the George, built in the same century as the church, the fifteenth. The George is indeed a real gem, with mullioned and bow windows, much half-timbering, a fine porch and a rear courtyard which is as interesting as the front of the building. The church is supposed to have been built by a man who was guided by nothing but his own inexperienced ingenuity, and there is certainly nothing like the tower anywhere in England.

Norton St Philip once claimed to have 'the most noted cloth fair in the West'. An upper room at the George was used as an exchange by the cloth merchants. The Duke of Monmouth also stayed here overnight prior to the battle of Sedgemoor and narrowly escaped death from the bullet of a would-be assassin, who fired at him through a window.

Returning across the hills to Bath we pass through Wellow, which was a manor of the Hungerford family. The fourteenth-century church was built by them, and their old manor still exists as a farm. In a garden near by is an ancient well, dedicated to St Julian. Several Roman villas have been discovered in the vicinity, including a large one with an excellent tesselated pavement excavated in 1822.

A mile to the south one can visit a remarkable long barrow at Stony Littleton. Excavated in 1816, it measures 107 feet by 54 feet by 13 feet high. Having entered through an entrance four feet high, the visitor can penetrate to the heart of the tumulus, passing through two large chambers, each six feet long by five wide, and seeing six other smaller rooms at the sides of the central passage.

All things agricultural are nowadays being crowded out of the Avon valley below Bath. The villages tend to link hands with each other and become dormitory suburbs for Bath and Bristol. Even Keynsham, an ancient town about midway between the two, has to fight to keep its identity.

Keynsham has sites of Roman villas, like most other places in this area. It was in existence, it seems, when Bladud was a swineherd (see page 42). In the sixth century a virgin princess named Keyna (hence the town's name) took up her residence here in a wild wood, and incidentally banished all poisonous snakes from it. In the Middle

Ages Keynsham had an abbey, the buildings of which were demolished to mend the roads in the reign of Henry VIII.

Keynsham has not been over-lucky. It lost its abbey; it lost a magnificent Roman pavement which was carted away to Bristol Museum; and it nearly lost its thirteenth-century church when the tower collapsed in a storm in 1632, doing much damage. Now it is being shaken to pieces by the thunder of heavy traffic.

4. Mendip

The primitive Celtic belief that certain hills were hollow and linked with a subterranean fairy world is understandable in Mendip. The villagers of Mendip, like the citizens of Bath, live on a kind of honeycomb, though here the rocky labyrinth beneath them is natural and not man-made. By diving into the nearest hole in the ground they may indeed discover a fantastic glittering realm of caverns and corridors, halls and swallets, brooks and waterfalls, where coloured rocks glistening with moisture and sparkling with reflective light seem to mirror grotesquely the familiar forms of the upper world, such as trees, spires, castles, domes, mushrooms and church organs.

An oval-shaped plateau rising at its highest point to 1,068 feet (at Black Down, about three miles north of Cheddar), the Mendips are wedged across north Somerset at right angles to the Cotswolds, with which they merge in their north-east sector. On the seaward end they taper off just south of Weston-super-Mare, with Brean Down and Steepholm as outlying fragments. From there to the neighbourhood of Frome, in the east, is about 20 miles, and the massif varies in breadth from about five to ten miles. On the north as well as on the east its boundaries are none-too-well demarcated, for swelling hills and deep valleys are the order of things until one reaches the Somerset frontier as defined by the Avon. On the southern side, however, the hills terminate abruptly in a steep scarp made the more dramatic by the dead-flat levels of the Somerset plain below.

The geological core of the Mendips is a mass of carboniferous limestone. This is a rock which slowly dissolves in water, or, to be more specific, is dissolved by the small amounts of carbonic acid contained in rainwater. The water, whether pouring down from aloft or welling up through saturated rock from below, naturally seeks the weakest and softest spots. So clefts and hollows are formed, and are enlarged into underground stream beds and spacious caves, until, in the course of geological time, the whole massif is as honeycombed as the interior of a sponge.

Wrapped around and dovetailed into the carboniferous limestone strata are measures of dolomitic conglomerate and old red sandstone, with some coal deposits in valleys in the north-east. Both the carboniferous limestone and the dolomitic conglomerate are veined with mineral ores, which have been extensively worked in times past and have contributed much to the character and history of Mendip.

High Mendip itself has no towns and few villages. Now that the miners have gone, the population stays down in the more congenial valleys and particularly in the towns and villages along the foot of the southern escarpment. Here, protected from the north by the great limestone wall, Axbridge, Cheddar, Wells, Shepton Mallet and a string of villages bask in sunshine. It is easy to see why the small farmers of the Cheddar district are able to specialize in early strawberries and anemones.

Winter is a quiet time on the Mendips. Anyone who enjoys the unpopular exercise of walking can spend a winter's day in complete solitude on the breezy uplands, while down below the growers protect their early crops with those strange, sausage-shaped balloons of plastic which make their rectangular fields look like fish-ponds. With spring, however, the tourists arrive, and the cult of holiday takes over Mendip.

The tour which takes in Bath, Cheddar and Wells in one day is popular. Not that one can do justice to Bath in a part of a day, but a sample is all that is asked. From Bath the cars and coaches pour down through Cheddar Gorge, probing here and there for parking space. Half an hour or so in one of the more spectacular caverns and then on to Wells and Wookey Hole.

Like the caves of Mendip, the Cheddar Gorge was formed by the action of water. Indeed, one theory maintains that it was originally a cave, the roof of which has collapsed. It is constructed on an impressive scale, a deep, sinuous cleft in the rocks, its walls rising as much as 480 feet above the valley floor (which is loftier than Salisbury Cathedral spire). Each turn of the road which climbs through the Gorge reveals new vistas of crags and pinnacles, festooned with trailing ivy, trees and ferns and so abrupt that one wonders whether the notices which warn of falling rock are not an understatement . . .

is not the whole crazy canyon in danger of collapse?

There have indeed been changes here within historical times. Henry of Huntingdon, who wrote between A.D. 1125 and 1130, includes among the wonders of England, 'Cheder Hole, where is a cavity under the earth, which, though many have often entered and there traversed great spaces of land, and rivers, they could yet never come to an end'. Holinshed, 300 years later, makes a similar statement. Nowadays the entrances by which one explores the caves at Cheddar no longer lead to any underground stream. Probably old entrances have been blocked by sediment and rocks washed down by flood water.

Floods were fairly frequent at Cheddar in the past, and a print of 200 years ago shows a torrent spreading right across the valley at the lower end of the Gorge. The lovely little lakes, linked by miniature waterfalls, and the surrounding gardens are a modern development. Cheddar town lies half a mile or so away from the entrance to the Gorge, on the road which runs, parallel to the Mendip escarpment, from Axbridge to Wells, and old pictures show few houses on the side road to the Gorge which all tourists now take.

The two main caves at Cheddar now open to the public, Gough's and Cox's, were both discovered in the nineteenth century. Cox's was found by a miller of that name who in 1837 pecked away at the rock face to make room for a new cartshed. Gough's Old Cave was apparently opened up or exploited by R. C. Gough in about 1877, though it was known before that to a couple named Jack and Nancy Beauchamp, who had a cottage near the entrance and used to charge visitors sixpence to walk through their garden to enter the cave. The Gough's Cave now visited by thousands every summer was exposed in the 1890s, at the expense of much hard digging by Mr Gough and his sons. A tremendous amount of work, involving the removal of debris from cave floors and blocked tunnels, the blasting of new access passages, the construction of pathways and bridges, and the installation of cunningly-placed electric lights, is necessary before the public can be admitted to a show cave. When it is finished visitors may stroll, hardly muddying their boots, through caverns formerly accessible only by means of much uncomfortable wriggling through slippery and restricted tunnels. And the fairyland of glistening stalactites and stalagmites which they see justifies the fanciful names, such as King Solomon's Temple, St Paul's, the Pixies' Forest and Aladdin's

Cave, which the exhibitors bestow on them.

Though the well-exploited caves at Cheddar are the best known, they are only samples of almost innumerable caverns under Mendip. An excellent little book, *The Complete Caves of Mendip*, published in 1970, lists over 420 of them. Almost every week-end cave-explorers are probing under Mendip, testing their skills on known descents and searching for new ones. There may well be caverns as spacious, spectacular and beautiful as any we have so far seen, still to be discovered, including some of which a tradition survives but which have been lost. An early nineteenth-century writer, J. Rutter, for instance, records a cave near Burrington Combe 'which was cal-culated to contain not less than one hundred skeletons', but no one now knows where it is.

Anyone wishing to explore subterranean Mendip should join one of the many caving clubs that operate in the region. This is no place for ill-equipped and inexperienced amateurs. Also, permits are re-quired to gain access to the mouths of most of the known caves. Among the many hazards is danger from sudden flooding, which is of frequent occurrence in this region of high rainfall and porous rock strata. Deaths have occurred through exposure, the victims being novices who ventured underground in light clothes and were trapped by rising water. A Mendip Rescue Organization has been formed to meet frequent calls for help.

The 'hundred skeletons' mentioned above serve as a reminder that the caves have been used by men from remote ages. They are indeed a happy hunting-ground for both archaeologists and palaeontologists.

Banwell Cave, near the western end of the Mendips, contains a curious wall of bones. It was built with meticulous care by a pioneer excavator, William Beard, early in the nineteenth century. The bones are those of mammoths, cave bears, cave lions, woolly rhinoceroses, hyenas, wolves, bisons and reindeers, which he found in huge quan-tities in the floor débris of the cave. A similar collection of pre-historic animal bones was discovered in a cave near Wookey, now known as the Hyena's Den. Here too were found traces of fibres made by prehistoric men, as well as bone and flint implements. This was one of the first sites in Britain to yield proofs that men were con-temporary with such animals as the cave bear and woolly rhinoceros.

As these well-protected animals of the receding Ice Age moved farther north in pursuit of the melting ice-cap, animals of a more temperate climate took their place. In Gough's cave, for example, human remains have been found with those of the red deer, roe deer and wild horses. So, starting with men of the Old Stone Age, for long centuries the caverns of Mendip were inhabited by families and clans of human beings. The caves would provide not only a ready-made roof over their heads and an equable temperature in summer and winter but also shelter and protection from enemies, both human and animal.

The caves were, in fact, not abandoned as human habitations until very recent times. Above Gough's cave at Cheddar is a cavern known as the Roman Cave, or Long Hole, which was evidently used extensively by Romano-British refugees in the Dark Ages—the fifth and sixth centuries, after the departure of the Roman legions. Large numbers of Roman coins, together with pots and other domestic articles and numerous weapons, have been found, indicating a retreat of the population from the open country below to the comparative safety of the cave, taking with them whatever valued possessions they could carry. There is evidence of fighting at the cave mouth.

Wookey Hole, second only to the Cheddar Gorge and Caves in popularity with tourists, offered even better amenities to human refugees. Here was a large cavern provided with not only a narrow and easily defended entrance but with a river of fresh water inside. The cavern which tourists see is a spacious hall, well endowed with stalactites and stalagmites, over the floor of which a lovely stream of clear, turquoise-blue water flows from its source far in the heart of Mendip. Beyond, however, are at least fourteen other chambers, accessible only to cavers with diving equipment, and more await discovery. One of the stalagmites is known as The Witch of Wookey, legend relating that she was an evil old woman turned to stone by the intervention of a monk from Glastonbury. The legend is very ancient, for it is recorded by a mediaeval writer, William of Worcester, who visited the cave in about 1470. 'There is also a chamber called an ost,' he writes, 'for the purpose of drying barley grain to make beer and so on, and the figure of a woman is there clad, and holding in her girdle a spinning distaff.' He also provides the information that 'at the beginning is an image of a man who goes by the name of the porter, and it is the duty of people who desire to enter the hall of Woky to ask permission of the porter, and they carry in their hands torches, which are called in English "shevys of reed-sedge", for the purpose of lighting up the hall'. Evidently Wookey Hole was much visited even in those days.

Strangely enough, or perhaps not so strangely, excavations at the cave entrance have revealed the skeleton of a woman, who seems to have been sacrificed, for near by was a sacrificial knife. Also buried with her were the bones of a goat and kid, an iron pot for holding milk and a kind of crystal ball of polished rock, so there may be some substance in the allegation that the cave was the home of a witch.

Not all the underground world of Mendip is of natural formation. From very early times the mineral wealth of the hills has been exploited. The plateau is disfigured by what Mendip people call 'gruffy ground' (from 'gruff', meaning a mine-shaft). The description given of it by F. A. Knight, writing in 1915, is accurate. The surface of the ground is, he wrote, 'in the roughest possible condition, . . . crowded with hollows and hillocks, . . . heaps of stony refuse and the mouths of old shafts'. Many of the caves of Mendip have been first discovered through mining operations.

The principal mineral mined in Mendip was lead. It is found here in the form of sulphide of lead, or galena, a lead-grey mineral found chiefly in veins in the carboniferous limestone. Old-time miners used to distinguish a number of different types of ore, some more valuable than others.

Another mineral which has been worked quite extensively is zinc, present in the form of zinc carbonate, or calamine. This was found in the dolomitic conglomerate rather than in the limestone.

The lead ores also contain small quantities of silver, which from early times was separated from the lead by a simple process known as cupellation. Lead melted in the open air quickly oxidizes, but any silver present does not, remaining on the surface of the lead oxide as a bead of pure metal.

Other minerals of which small quantities have been mined on Mendip are manganese, iron and copper. Outside the strict limits of the Mendip hills, though within the area we are now considering, are considerable deposits of coal, exploited commercially till 1973. Some small coal measures have also been found in the carboniferous limestone of Mendip proper. Small amounts of barium, in the form of barium sulphate, were mined in the nineteenth century. Without doubt the Mendips contain other mineral deposits, quite possibly of some of the rarer elements for which they have never been thoroughly explored and for which we are only now beginning to find uses.

Whether lead was being mined on Mendip before the Roman invasion we do not know, but the likelihood is that it was. The Roman legions landed in A.D. 43, and by A.D. 49 the lead mines were in full operation. Two pigs of lead of that date, one weighing 163 pounds, have been found on Mendip, one near Wookey Hole and the other near Blagdon. The first bears an inscription which, translated, reads: 'The property of Tiberius Claudius Caesar Augustus, Pontifex Maximus, holder of the Tribunician power for the ninth time, Imperator for the sixteenth time. From Britain.'

Which, of course, dates it accurately.

The Romans could hardly have been so quick off the mark if they had not known of the existence of mineral ores in the Mendips. It may well be that lead was one of the chief prizes they hoped to gain by their invasion of the West Country. Before their time leaden objects, including weights for fishing nets, were in use in the lake villages of lowland Somerset, and certain British states had a silver coinage. Both lead and silver probably came from within Britain, and where more likely than Mendip?

The Mendip mines seem to have been worked throughout the Roman period, the centre of activity being around Charterhouse, where numerous Roman remains, including many coins, have been found. The mines are thought to have been all surface workings, for no deep shafts have been discovered. Doubtless the work was done by slave labour.

Although the Saxons used lead for church roofs and other purposes and must have mined it somewhere, we have no further direct evidence of the mines being worked until the twelfth century, when Richard I granted a mining charter to the Bishop of Bath. A hundred years later, in 1283, a permit to work lead mines on an extensive area of land granted them on Mendip was given to the new Carthusian monastery at Witham Friary (see page 37). This must have been around Charterhouse, which, of course, derives its name from the Carthusians. Lead mining continued throughout the Middle Ages, and there are fourteenth-century records of a thriving export trade from Bristol in lead, much of which probably came from Mendip. Some silver also seems to have been produced about this time.

As with the tin mines of Devon and Cornwall, which had their Stannary laws, the Mendip mines evolved their own code of laws, doubtless based on custom. The laws are first set out in a document purporting to have been drafted in the reign of Edward IV but probably belonging to later Tudor times. They define the terms by which a man could establish mining rights, the extent of those rights and the rules he must observe in exercising them. A great deal of valuable topographical information is recorded incidentally.

In Saxon and early mediaeval times most of the summit of Mendip was apparently classed as a royal forest. At some time during the Middle Ages, probably in the late fourteenth century, the royal rights passed to four Lords Royal, who were local gentry or other magnates (the Abbot of Glastonbury may have been one). In their respective divisions of Mendip they held their own courts and were responsible for maintaining the laws, customs, rights and privileges of the mines and commons.

Intermediate between the Lord Royal and the miners stood the lead-reeve, an official appointed from the more affluent local peasants, merchants or farmers. His duty was to see that the rules were kept by the miners and, more particularly, to collect from them the 10 per cent due to the lord. Records of Tudor and Stuart times abound in details of disputes concerning lead-reeves. Much of the evidence suggests that to hold the office was a burden rather than an advantage, and many eligible candidates attempted to evade election. On the other hand, some lead-reeves seem to have made a very good thing of it, and some paid a premium in order to be re-appointed. One supposes that the profit depended on the degree of corruption that the reeve was prepared to practise.

Mining was evidently a solitary or family affair. We do not hear of communally-worked mines. The individual miners were also responsible for delivering their ore to the smelting works, which were owned by a Lord Royal.

By the end of the seventeenth century most of the easily accessible lodes had been worked out, and the miners were having to penetrate deeper below ground, where they frequntly ran into trouble with floods. During the Napoleonic Wars lead mining, as always with a home industry in wartime, enjoyed moderate prosperity, but with peace came a cut in the import duty on lead. Coupled with the increasing practical difficulties of deep mining, this virtually killed the ancient industry on Mendip. By 1830 lead mining had almost ceased.

Mendip miners had, however, a reserve on which to fall back. Zinc, for mixing with copper to make brass, was in strong demand in the factories of Bristol. The mining of calamine, the ore which yields zinc, began in Mendip in the reign of Elizabeth I. In the eighteenth century several of the Mendip villages, notably Row-berrow, Wrington and Shipham, were populated almost exclusively by calamine miners. Extracting calamine ore proved profitable for longer than lead mining, but in the end the same circumstance, namely the availability of cheaper supplies from overseas, doomed it to extinction. The industry had ceased by about the middle of the nineteenth century, although for 50 years afterwards schemes for reviving it continued to be assiduously but vainly discussed.

Manganese was another mineral mined on Mendip. It occurs there chiefly in the form of manganese dioxide, or pyrolusite, known to our ancestors as 'pottern-ore'. The name was given it because it was in considerable demand by potters, who used it for colouring earthenware black. Extraction of manganese ore seems to have begun in the mid-seventeenth century and to have continued, off and on, till 1891. The industry was, however, never large.

Iron ores, in the form of red ochre and yellow ochre, are found in various parts of Mendip and adjacent areas of north Somerset. The earliest reference to iron being mined there is as far back as 1235. Ochre miners seem to have been fairly active in the region throughout the centuries, and ochre is still being mined, or was until recently, though for paint rather than for iron. Ochre veins in the Mendips are numerous and often rich but tend to be short-lived.

The other incidental, though perhaps to term it so is hardly just, is the daily life of the miners themselves. In general we have little information on the daily life of the miners, few writers until modern times ever considering it worth while to record the lives of ordinary folk. The first real shaft of light falls on them in the writings of Hannah More and her sister Martha, who were two of five daughters of a Bristol schoolmaster.

Hannah is remembered chiefly as an indefatigable writer of religious tracts, which strike us as being soupily sentimental, but she was an able practitioner with the pen and produced several plays, essays and books. Born in 1755, she was an early example of the

Victorian philanthropist, devoted to good works among the poor; but we would be wrong to allow any prejudice on that account to detract from our appreciation of the sustained and self-sacrificing efforts she made to improve the lot of the Mendip miners. Her sister Martha wrote:

'Among the most depraved and wretched were Shipham and Row-berrow, two mining villages at the top of Mendip; the people savage and depraved almost even beyond Cheddar, brutal in their natures, and ferocious in their manners. They began by suspecting we should make our fortunes by selling their children as slaves. No constable would venture to arrest a Shipham man, lest he should be concealed in one of their pits, and never heard of more; no uncommon case.'

Hannah started Sunday Schools, some saving clubs which she called 'Female Friendly Societies' knitting classes and sundry other benefit organizations. She marshalled local philanthropic forces, and her religious tracts sold, nationwide, two million copies in a single year. Great improvements were affected on Mendip, yet nearly 50 years later a Rev. Henry Thompson was able to record visiting 'the last surviving inhabitant of a *cave* in the Cheddar cliffs', and her environment gives a glimpse of what must have been common conditions at an earlier date.

'The abode, far better adapted for a sepulchre than a dwelling, extended a considerable distance into the rock. A narrow fissure served to carry off the smoke, while the inner part of the cavern, ceiled with stalactites, was on every side dripping with damp. A rough wooden door rudely following the outline of the cavern's mouth was the only protection against external violence. In this habitation a human being had existed for upwards of thirty years. This woman, wild and squalid as her dwelling, was only one individual of a class who although inhabiting more humanizing abodes were neither less ignorant nor less barbarous. Females, whom nothing less but their female garb could associate in the traveller's mind with an idea of the sex, hung on his path at every step, vending the mineral productions of the country and the seeds of the Cheddar pink, and not infrequently engaging in furious and even sanguinary contention when any of the unsightly sisterhood appeared to have been more successful in such attempts than the rest.'

The realities of cave-dwelling must have been much like this in all ages.

The coal measures of north Somerset are on the fringe of Mendip, between the massif proper and Bath. Visitors familiar with the grim industrial setting of coal mines in the north are surprised at the rural appearance of the Somerset coalfield. The slag-heaps rise against a background of vivid green pastures, and the mining centres of Radstock, Midsomer Norton and Farringdon Gurney are little more than large villages. Reference to them should, however, be made in the past tense. The last mine closed in the autumn of 1973, after a gradual but steady decline of the industry since the First World War. Then the Somerset mines were employing over 7,000 men and producing over a million tons of coal a year, but one by one the pits have closed.

The problems are economic. Coal is still there, but in tortuous and distorted seams which make the operation of coal-face machinery difficult. Also the quality is not high, most of the coal being suitable only for industrial use. In time of urgent need, the pits could be reopened and more coal won.

No one knows when Mendip coal was first exploited, but the rents paid for mines to landowners are recorded early in the fourteenth century. As with the mining of mineral ores in the district, the first in the field were local peasants who augmented their income by drift mining, extracting what coal they could from shallow quarries. The coal was taken for centuries in panniers, horseback, to towns and villages within reasonable distance but chiefly to Bath.

As the mines struck deeper more mechanical aids, such as engines powered by water-mills, were required and better organization demanded. In the great age of canal-building, in the eighteenth century, two waterways to convey Mendip coal to the outer world were attempted. One, the Dorset and Somerset Canal, which was designed to carry the coal via Frome to the towns and villages of north Dorset, was never completed. The other, the Somerset Coal Canal, after many difficulties, did indeed function, though the final section, nearest Radstock, was replaced by a railway, on which first horse-drawn and then steam-drawn trucks were used. The hilly terrain necessitated the construction of 22 locks in one section alone of the canal, near Combe Hay. This Canal joined the Kennet and Avon Canal and so provided a waterway link with London and with the canal system of the Midlands. Later, the railways took over from the canals, and the second

half of the nineteenth century was a period of considerable prosperity for the Mendip coalfield. Railways, mines and ironworks have
now all closed.

The fact that so far in this chapter we have been dealing with underground Mendip should not lead to the supposition that nothing of
importance or interest happened on the surface. The Mendip region
can be conveniently divided into three sections: the Mendip plateau;
the hilly, serrated country to the north and east; and the string
of villages and little towns under the southern edge of the escarpment.

The plateau itself, with an average elevation of about 800 feet, is
an austere, inhospitable place, its few villages and isolated farms
cowering in whatever shelter they can find. Stone walls constructed
of rocks mostly picked up from the thin-soiled fields make a network of pastures, the walls serving not only as boundaries but also
as shelter for the sheep, which are the predominant animals. Until
the middle of the eighteenth century this was nearly all common
land. After the enclosure acts, some of it was ploughed, as it has been
at various subsequent periods. During the 1939–45 war fields even
on the top of Mendip grew quite creditable crops of potatoes, barley
and even wheat. But when national emergencies subside, Mendip
reverts to its natural coarse grass. Ripening and harvesting other
crops is too precarious on those rainswept, misty heights.

Mendip is traditionally given over to sheep, though now they are
interspersed with young cattle, being reared for lowland dairies, and
a few milking herds. Sheep have grazed the downs from time immemorial, the pivot of the shepherds' year being Priddy Fair, for the
dispersal of the season's crop of lambs. A thatched stack of hurdles,
for use in penning the sheep, stands all the year round on the village
green. Tradition has it that the Fair was moved up to Priddy from
Wells in about 1348 or 1349, in an attempt to escape the ravages of
the Black Death. The story is possible, but I am inclined to doubt it.
Most of the hilltop fairs originated in prehistoric times. They provided focal points in the calendar of the Iron Age folk who lived in
the turf-walled villages round about. High Mendip in those days
probably had a considerable population, for all around Priddy are
earthworks, hill 'forts' and other traces of ancient habitation, includ-

7   *Glastonbury: the fifteenth-century George and Pilgrims Inn*

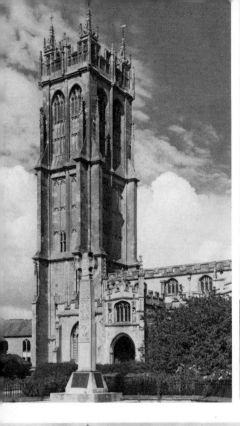

ing what is supposed to be a Roman amphitheatre; also numerous barrows.

Priddy Fair retains much of its ancient character, it being a fair in most senses of the word, besides being an exchange mart for sheep. Here are stalls and cheap-jacks, catering vans and ice-cream vans, and stands for selling agricultural equipment and clothing. The entertainment aspect is lacking, however, and it is no longer a hiring fair.

Memory of the flourishing wool trade of the Middle Ages is perpetuated in the name of the Mendip village of Charterhouse. The place was founded in the reign of Henry III as a 'colony' of the Carthusian monastery of Witham Friary (see page 65). Doubtless the monks had much to do with the development of good sheep farming and the wool trade, though the wool seems mostly to have been taken to the foot of the hills, to Frome, Mells, Wells and other places, for spinning and weaving. Robert Trow-Smith, in his *History of British Livestock Husbandry*, states that early mediaeval records also reveal large numbers of goats on Mendip (50 she-goats at Chewton Mendip and 68 at Rodney Stoke, for instance, according to the Domesday Book). They would presumably feed on the steep, bush-clad hillsides and ravines.

In mediaeval times much of Mendip and the surrounding countryside was classified as a Royal Forest. The term 'forest' is, of course, somewhat misleading, for it does not imply that Mendip was forested. The word 'Chase' is perhaps better; the territory was reserved for the king's hunting, and the severe forest laws codified by William the Conqueror were applied. Not only deer but even such lesser animals as rabbits, squirrels and wild bees were rigidly protected, and villagers who managed to exist within the forest boundaries had to pay handsomely for rights of pasture and woodgathering. The history of the Middle Ages is studded with records of attempts to extend such rights, and also with lively stories of poaching affrays.

The site of the ancient Saxon hunting lodge at Axbridge is now occupied by a building known as King John's Hunting Lodge, which dates not from King John's time but from the early sixteenth century. King John was, however, often here, as were most other mediaeval kings. In the thirteenth and early fourteenth centuries the borough used to send two members to Parliament. The oldest build-

8 *Church Towers of: St John's Glastonbury (Top left); Bruton (Top right); Weston Zoyland (Bottom left); Chewton Mendip (Bottom right)*

ing in the town is the church, of fifteenth-century date and Perpendicular style. Like so many other Somerset churches, it has a fine central tower; also, a splendid panelled roof to the nave.

Tragedy struck Axbridge and neighbouring villages in the spring of 1973 when a plane carrying many of the women on a day's excursion to Switzerland crashed on the outskirts of Basle, with great loss of life.

In the quiet centuries which followed its mediaeval era of importance Axbridge developed its early vegetable industry, for which its soil and its climate (on the southern side of the protective scarp of Mendip) eminently suit it. This horticultural speciality is intensified as one travels along the foot of the cliffs, eastwards from Axbridge. Sloping fields between the road and the hills are planted with rows of strawberries, anemones, carrots and other specialities, protected in late winter and early spring by acres of plastic, which look as though the streams of subterranean Mendip had burst out and expanded into shining pools. Cheddar is the centre of the industry, Cheddar strawberries, ripe in May and early June, having become almost as celebrated as Cheddar cheese. Strawberry-growing in the district dates from about 1870. About 300 growers are engaged in it, most of them having small holdings of less than 20 acres, and the fruit is sent, mainly by road nowadays, to most of the big towns of Britain.

Cheese-making is a much older Cheddar industry. It was certainly flourishing in the sixteenth century, for William Camden, writing in 1586, mentions that Cheddar is 'famous for the excellent and prodigious great cheeses made there, some of which require more than a man's strength to set them on the table'. At an earlier time it seems likely that cheese was made locally chiefly from sheep's milk, as was a widespread practice. Scholars who have studied the Domesday Book have noted that the Royal manor of Cheddar possessed not a single cow in 1086, though large numbers of sheep were kept in the district.

Daniel Defoe, who visited the West Country in 1722, before the flood of enclosure acts, was impressed by the Cheddar cheese-makers. Although the cows were individually owned, he records, they were kept on a communal basis as a town herd:

'Before the village is a large green, or common, a piece of ground, in which the whole herd of the cows, belonging to the town, do feed; the ground is exceedingly rich, and as the whole village are cowkeepers, they take care to keep up the goodness of the soil, by agreeing to lay on large quantities of dung for manuring, and in-riching the land.

'The milk of all the town cows, is brought together every day into a common room, where the persons appointed, or trusted for the management, measure every man's quantity, and set it down in a book; when the quantities are adjusted, the milk is all put to-gether, and every meal's milk makes one cheese, and no more; so that the cheese is bigger, or less, as the cows yield more, or less, milk. By this method the goodness of the cheese is preserved, and, without all dispute, it is the best cheese that England affords, if not, that the whole world affords.'

The fact that 'the whole village were cow-keepers' accounts for the fact that the little town of Cheddar turns its back on the Gorge, the best part of a mile away, and faces the mid-day sun. The attrac-tions of the Gorge have become fashionable only in comparatively recent times, much more recent than the fifteenth-century market cross around which Cheddar clusters. Its church of St Andrew, in early Perpendicular style, has another of those splendid towers, 110 feet high, with beautiful stone tracery and elegant pinnacles. Also like many other Somerset churches, it has a fine stone pulpit of the fifteenth century, a feature unusual in most other parts of England.

Cheddar was a royal manor in the time of Alfred the Great, being mentioned in his will. Roman coins have been found here, and the palaeolithic skeleton, discovered in one of the caves and known as the Cheddar Man, may have belonged to an individual who lived 20,000 years ago.

Nine miles south-eastwards from Cheddar, along the foot of the Mendip cliffs, the thriving little town of Wells has been elevated by its cathedral to city status. Leland, in the sixteenth century, records that 'the toune of Welles is sette yn the rootes of Mendepe Hille in a stony soile and ful of springes, whereof it hath the name'; and it is also recorded that a church which was already standing on the site of the present cathedral in 909, when King Edward the Elder chose it for a new bishopric, was situated near 'the great fountain of St Andrew'.

The first church, or shrine, was apparently built here about A.D. 700 by King Ina, of Wessex. Wells continued as the seat of a bishopric throughout Saxon times and until the reign of William Rufus, when, as we have noted on page 47, the Norman bishop John of Tours moved his seat to Bath. The old cathedral church at Wells was pulled down. Trouble naturally followed, and in 1206 a compromise solution decreed that the bishopric should henceforth be known as that of Bath and Wells.

Bishop Jocelyn, who was elevated to the see in 1206, decided to live at Wells and built the Bishop's Palace in which twentieth-century bishops still live. He was likewise responsible for much of the cathedral, including the magnificent west front and the nave. The west front of Wells Cathedral, with its rank upon rank of sculptured figures—saints, apostles, prophets, martyrs culminating in the figure of Christ Himself—is one of the glories of English architecture. Equally memorable are the soaring inverted arches which help to support the weight of the central tower and which foster the impression that the cathedral has sprung up naturally from the Somerset soil; as, in a sense, it has, for the Doulting quarries which provided the stone are less than seven miles distant. Doulting stone, a lovely creamy white when freshly cut, unfortunately weathers badly, and so the cathedral slowly crumbles and is in almost constant need of repair. Many of the statues on the west face have lost their features through exposure, in addition to several in the lower tiers which the Duke of Monmouth's men knocked about in 1685.

The inverted arches, incidentally, were not an original feature of the cathedral but were added in 1337 when the central tower, built on waterlogged ground, showed signs of collapse.

A spectacular feature of the cathedral, beloved by children, is the Wells Clock. Seated beside it Jack Blandiver at every quarter of an hour kicks two bells with his heels. On the hour four mounted knights come charging out, knocking each other off their horses. This ingenious piece of mechanism, which shows not only the hours and minutes but the days of the month and the phases of the moon, was made by a Glastonbury monk, Peter Lightfoot, in 1325, or by one of his pupils.

Looked at from whatever angle, Wells Cathedral speaks to the imagination. The north porch is almost as rich in carving as is the west face, as also are the capitals of the pillars in the nave and transepts and the misereres in the choir stalls. Mediaeval craftsmen in wood and stone let their imaginations run riot in Wells. We can find, if we look carefully, a girl digging a thorn from her foot, two dragons biting each other's tails, a man with the toothache, a robber caught stealing fruit, a shoemaker at his work, and many other facets of mediaeval life. Sunbeams are split prismatically by an abundance of fine stained glass, including a Jesse window.

Outside, the setting of the cathedral, in a close of spacious lawns, is superb. One can always be finding new angles from which to admire it. It is but one, although the chief one, of a whole complex of mediaeval buildings. From the north transept a flight of stone steps lead to the airy, octagonal chapter-house. Beyond is the fifteenth-century deanery, where King Henry VII once feasted.

On the other side of the cathedral a gateway, known as the Palace Eye, leads to the Bishop's Palace, a squat, massive building looking much as Bishop Jocelyn must have left it. The moat around it is a later addition but even so is well over 500 years old. Here an attraction is the swans which, for over 100 years, have practised the trick of pulling at a bell-rope for food when hungry.

Other architectural features of Wells are the Bishop's Barn, a large fifteenth-century edifice, several almshouses, and the sixteenth-century Crown Inn, overlooking the market place. Visitors approaching Wells from the direction of Cheddar sometimes mistake St Cuthbert's Church, when seen from a distance, for the cathedral. St Cuthbert's is indeed well worth a visit. Erected at different periods, some of the earliest work dating from the thirteenth century, it has an imposing tower and is said to be the largest parish church in Somerset.

The history of Wells is bound up with that of the cathedral. Throughout the Middle Ages, the Bishop of Bath and Wells was constantly at loggerheads with the Abbot of Glastonbury, and no doubt their bickerings were to some extent enjoyed by the townsfolk. In the Civil War the sympathies of Wells, predictably in a cathedral city, lay with the Royalists, and, the rest of Somerset being mainly Puritan, Wells had to endure quite a bit of buffeting by marauding troops.

The road along which rumbling carts brought Doulting stone for the building of Wells Cathedral, palaces, battlements and gatehouses passed through Shepton Mallet, the fourth and last of the towns along the southern fringe of Mendip. 'Shepton' is 'sheep-town', and Mallet, or Malet, the name of the family to whom the manor belonged in the twelfth century.

Like so many villages and towns in these parts, Shepton began its life as an outlying estate of the Abbot of Glastonbury, to whom land was first granted here by the West Saxon king Ina in A.D. 706. It rose to outstanding prosperity from the fourteenth century onwards as a wool town. The industry received a new impetus by the settlement here, in the last quarter of the sixteenth century, of Huguenot refugees. And by 1790 it is said that no fewer than 4,000 people were employed in the wool trade in Shepton Mallet, which was obviously then one of the largest towns in the West of England.

Soon after that, however, manufacturing industry moved from the south-west to northern England. Shepton Mallet gradually lost its factories and sank to the pleasanter status of a country market town, which it still is. In the Civil War, Shepton Mallet came early to the forefront, it being the scene of one of the first confrontations, bloodless as it happened, between the supporters of King and Parliament. This was in the August of 1642, before the war had properly started. Again in Monmouth's Rebellion Shepton Mallet contributed men and money to the Duke's cause and was visited by Monmouth both on his triumphal outward march and on his tragic retreat.

Shepton Mallet's great church was built for the town by wool merchants in the fifteenth century, probably on the site of a Saxon church. Apart from its fine tower, its most notable feature is its magnificent oaken waggon roof, said by some experts to be the finest in England. Its 350 carved panels and nearly 400 carved bosses are all of different designs.

For centuries the commercial and social life of Shepton Mallet centred on its Market Cross, erected in 1500 and still standing. Near by are a surviving section of the mediaeval Shambles, which are tiled roofs supported by sturdy timbers and sheltering market benches. Though 'shambles' is generally taken to refer to slaughter-houses, its meaning here is 'market stalls'. The Shambles were Shepton Mallet's mediaeval version of a supermarket!

Shepton Mallet also has a prison, built about the year 1624 and still used for certain types of prisoners. An execution took place there as late as 1926. Its agricultural show has been amalgamated with that of the Bath & West, which now has a permanent site a mile or so south of the town. Among the modern industries which flourish in the neighbourhood one of the best-known is the perry-making factory where Showerings bottle 'Babycham'.

In our rapid journey from Axbridge to Shepton Mallet we have by-passed numerous attractive villages, and more stud the country-side to the east, north and west of the Mendip massif. Most of them are set like jewels among tall trees in lovely valleys, often by spark-ling streams or still pools. Here we visit a few of the more interest-ing, though it is worth reminding ourselves that some of those which have nothing spectacular to commend them may be most rewarding in their aura of peace and serenity.

Hard by Shepton Mallet runs the ancient Fosse Way. A few miles farther along the road to Bath lies the village of Stratton-on-the-Fosse, dominated by the mighty Benedictine abbey of Downside. Like many of Somerset's light industries, it was founded by refugees. After the Reformation in England monks of the Benedictine order fled to France, where for more than 200 years they lived at Douai. The French Revolution set them on their travels again, and they returned to England, to find eventually, in 1814, a permanent home at Stratton-on-the-Fosse. The Abbey, vast and imposing with a tower that can be seen from far and wide, attracts thousands of visitors every year. It has a magnificent church, with a remarkable organ, and its associated school has a world-wide reputation.

A few miles to the east, on the Frome road, Mells is one of the love-liest villages in Somerset—'a show place'. Here are pleasant stone cottages, amid gardens and trees, set around a splendid sixteenth-century church with a tower more than 100 feet high. Here for centuries was the home of the Horner family, the last heir of which was killed at the battle of Cambrai in 1917. Sir Alfred Munnings de-signed the fine equestrian statue of young Edward Horner which may be seen in the Horner chapel of the church.

Mells was also the home of a notable family of ironmasters, the Fussells, who were making edged tools there as early as 1744. So prosperous were they in the first half of the nineteenth century that their mills were springing up like mushrooms in the neighbouring villages, to the consternation of the Horner family, who saw the industrial revolution with its accompanying devastation of the countryside happening on their own doorstep. The prolonged legal battles and financial negotiations between the Fussells and the Horners, principal landowners in the district, make interesting reading. The ironworks declined with the depression of agriculture, for which it made tools, in the 1870s. Now all that remains of Mells iron industry are the Fussells' house, the Chantry and numerous ruins of ironworks, dammed streams, derelict cottages and rubbish pits in the valleys around the village.

Another industry which flourished extensively in the Mendip country in the eighteenth and nineteenth centuries was paper-making which, in the words of an early expert, requires 'quick streams and clear water'. Mendip, with its streams gushing straight from subterranean caverns, has, of course, an abundance of both. The largest surviving establishment is the flourishing paper mill at Wookey Hole, which was founded in the sixteenth century, one of the first in England. Most of the Mendip paper-mills, being small-scale enterprises operated mostly by manual labour, have vanished, though traces of the buildings which housed them may still be found at Banwell, Cheddar, Stoke Bottom and elsewhere. The Wookey Hole mills, however, go from strength to strength and now supply a wide range of quality paper, much of it for export.

In this quarter of Somerset small local industries such as brewing, quarrying and, of course, the mining of coal and minerals, proliferated, particularly in the eighteenth centuries. Industrial archaeologists spend happy week-ends exploring secluded valleys and forgotten combes for relics of the past activities and in tracing the lines of the little railways which once served the mills and mines. Oakhill, near Shepton Mallet, for example, once had a brewery with an output of up to 2,500 barrels of stout and beer weekly. To serve it a handsome little private railway, with a $2\frac{1}{2}$-feet gauge, was built from Oakhill to Binegar, where it linked up with the Somerset and Dorset Joint Railway. Robert Atthill, in his book *Old Mendip*, describes how the 'two sturdy little saddle-tank engines, *Mendip* and *Oakhill*, hauled trains of long, low trucks piled with barrels, on which the village children delighted to ride'.

At the other end of Mendip the large village of Banwell was another Mendip location for a paper mill, which once made paper for Bank of England notes. Even the mill pool, a lovely pond with an island and swans, in the middle of the village, has since been drained.

Also in this western section of Mendip is Burrington, below which a combe, or ravine, cleaves deep into the heart of the escarpment.

Here a carved inscription on a rock reminds us that the Rev. Augustus Toplady, curate of Blagdon, wrote the hymn 'Rock of Ages' while sheltering there from a storm in 1762.

At Blagdon, near by, we enter the Somerset lake district, a series of man-made lakes constructed to supply Bristol with water. Blagdon Lake, or Yeo Reservoir, covers about 450 acres; Chew Reservoir, a few miles to the east, 1,200 acres. On the south side of the hills another large reservoir has been constructed between Cheddar and Axbridge. The northern lakes are fringed with trees and enhance rather than detract from the landscape. All are bountifully stocked with fish and attract large numbers of waterfowl. There is a trout hatchery by Blagdon Lake and a bird-ringing station by Chew Reservoir.

To return yet again to those noble church towers, there are splendid ones at Wrington, Chew Magna, Chew Stoke, Chewton Mendip, Winscombe and Leigh-on-Mendip. Another, at Dundry, thrusts up from Dundry Hill, which is an outlying island of Mendip, beyond the Chew valley. From it one can look down on Bristol, creeping up over the slopes of the Avon valley and its tributaries, and beyond that to the Severn Sea and Wales.

Here, along this northern fringe of Mendip, are pleasant little villages with intriguing names such as Nempnett Thrubwell, Ubley and Temple Cloud. Scarcely a parish church but has some feature worth examining.

Before we leave the region, however, we must take note of an edifice that antedates any churches, cathedrals, factories, mines or even the villages themselves. In a field by Stanton Drew, a couple of miles east of Chew Magna, the Standing Stones may well be as old as Stonehenge or Avebury. The stones, which average about six feet in height, are arranged in three circles, the largest of which, the Great Circle, is 368 feet across. Associated with it is another group of stones, in the shape of a horse-shoe, known as The Cove, which may have been the chamber of a long barrow. Six hundred yards away is an isolated stone known as Hauteville's Quoit.

Their purpose is unknown, though archaeologists suspect that they served some sort of ritual. John Wood, the Bath antiquary whom we have met in Chapter 3, recorded his own version of their significance:

'No one, say the country people about Stantondrue, was ever able to reckon the number of these metamorphosed stones, or to take a draught of them, though several have attempted to do both, and proceeded till they were either struck dead upon the spot, or with such illness as soon carried them off.'

The word 'metamorphosed' refers to the local legend that the stones are wedding guests who continued their dancing so late on a Saturday night that they overlapped into the Sabbath, whereupon the Devil, who was accompanying them disguised as a fiddler, turned them into stone. One day, he said, he would come back to play to them again, and then they would resume their dance.

I have counted the Standing Stones and make the number twenty-seven.

5. Glastonbury

As the storms sweep in from the west, my neighbours in the little village on the Ilchester levels where I live as I write this book, remark sagely:

'Ah, we shall miss that lot. They're going around Glastonbury way.'

Or, surveying a promising litter of pigs, they will say:

'Reckon they can go to Glastonbury next week. Tid'n a bad market for pigs, Glastonbury.'

Such is the mild impact of Glastonbury on twentieth-century life in Somerset. A location under the hills which the storms follow. A fairly good market for pigs. It's enough to bring back from the grave, in outraged majesty, those regal Abbots of Glastonbury who once ruled like monarchs over half the West Country.

'If the Abbot of Glastonbury were to marry the Abbess of Shaftesbury', commented some of our irreverent forefathers, 'their first-born would own more land than the King of England.'

And before that age of wealth and ostentatious glory, the mystery and holiness of the most numinous site in Britain. Traditions, legends, conjecture, fancies, cluster around Glastonbury like swarming bees around a queen. The mystical and esoteric mingle with the commonplace. As recently as 1972/73 the worthy tradesmen of Glastonbury endured disapprovingly the descent of a colony of free-thinkers, mostly of the 'hippy' type, who indulged in vegetarianism, long hair, outlandish clothes and a medley of nebulous but vaguely alarming tenets.

Everyday Glastonbury is indeed in a dilemma. Like Stratford-on-Avon, it is overwhelmed by its past. Glastonbury is put on the map by its history. Much of its present prosperity depends on its catering for tourists, to catch whose custom local commerce has developed 'Avalon' as a kind of trademark. You can buy Avalon baskets and coats, fill your car with petrol at an Avalon garage and sip tea at an Avalon café. But how to differentiate between those visitors who have money and those who have not? Nowadays dress is no infallible clue. And how to endure the constant disapproval of tourists who, expecting something in keeping with the past grandeur of the place, are disappointed by the lack of almost anything impressive in the town itself and by the predominance of suburban houses which might belong anywhere and which, in a country of abundant building-stone, are mostly constructed of red brick? Glastonbury's natural desire is to be left alone, to get on with its business; then comes the realization that catering for tourism *is* its business.

The visitors come to see the ruins of the vast mediaeval Abbey. They inspect the Glastonbury Thorn, which bears its flowers at Christmas-time. They walk up the road to peer into the Chalice Well (if they can find it, for Glastonbury is not particularly efficient at signposting its treasures). Then on to the foot of the Tor, a pyramidal hill crowned by a ruined tower. Climbing to the summit needs a tranquil summer day. when it can be a pleasant expedition, rewarded by the significant panorama in all directions. The Abbey's tithe barn and the Glastonbury museum may also be visited, if time allows.

The ruins of the Abbey itself are now set in well-kept lawns surrounded by a stone precinct wall. One naturally pays to enter and hands over more cash for a guide-book. The features of the place are clearly and neatly labelled, so the imagination is well provided with nourishment.

The chief impression is of size. The Abbey itself was 594 feet long, more than 200 feet longer than Wells Cathedral. The roof of the nave towered 100 feet above floor level. The transepts measured 175 feet. Reconstructions of the place show a massive rather than elegant building.

All, of course, is now ruinous. Sightless windows, their stained glass smashed long ago, would, if they could see, have nothing to look down upon save acres of grass and vaults now open to the sky. The only building surviving intact is the so-called Abbot's Kitchen, an octagonal structure which was probably a refectory where guests ate. What happened to the rest of the huge fabric is illustrated by the testimony of William Stukely who, writing in the 1720s says:

'As yet there are magnificent ruins, but within a lustrum of years a Presbyterian tenant has made more barbarous havoc there than had been since the dissolution; for every week a pillar or buttress, a window jamb or an angle of fine hewn stone is sold to the best bidder. While I was there they were excoriating St Joseph's Chapel for that purpose, and the squared stones were laid up by lots in the Abbot's Kitchen; the rest goes to paving yards and stalls for cattle, or to the highway.'

It was but one iconoclastic period, though perhaps the worst, among many that transpired after the dissolution of the Abbey in 1539. The process started as soon as the last Abbot was safely hanged. Gangs of workmen descended upon the place and stripped the roof of lead, using priceless carved wooden screens as fuel to melt it down and ancient manuscripts to kindle the fires.

Now the Abbey has a respite from destruction. It belongs to the Church of England, who keep the premises in excellent repair. The old Catholic pilgrimage to Our Lady of Glastonbury has been revived. Morality plays, with music and dance, are performed within the ruins. And the little town thrives on its visitors.

Having thus briefly surveyed modern Glastonbury and the ruins which link it with the past, we ask ourselves, Why such a fuss about an obscure little town in the Somerset marshes? How did such an important abbey come to be built there? And what is the significance of that oddly shaped Tor?

It is difficult to answer these questions at all satisfactorily, for, no matter how far back we delve, there is always something at Glastonbury. Abbot Richard Whiting, who was hanged on the Tor in 1539, was reputed to be the sixtieth abbot of Glastonbury.

William of Malmesbury, a scholar monk of no mean ability, visited Glastonbury early in the twelfth century, perhaps in the 1120s or 1130s. In his *History of the Kings of England* he writes:

'Willingly would I declare the meaning of those pyramids, which are almost incomprehensible to all, could I but ascertain the truth. These, situated some few feet from the church, border on the cemetery of the monks. That which is the loftiest and nearest the church is 28 feet high and has five storeys; this, though threatening ruin from its extreme age, possesses nevertheless some traces of antiquity, which may be clearly read though not perfectly understood. In the highest storey is an image in a pontifical habit. In the next, a statue of regal dignity, and the letters Her Sexi and Blisperh. In the third, too, are the names, Penerest, Bantomp, Pinepegn. In the fourth, Bate, Pulfred and Eanfled. In the fifth, which is the lowest, there is an image, and the words as follow, Logor, Peslicas, and Bregden, Spelpes, Highingendes Bearn. The other pyramid is 26 feet high and has four storeys, in which are read Kentwin, Hedda the bishop, and Bregored, and Beorward. The meaning of these I do not hastily decide, but I shrewdly conjecture that within, in stone coffins, are contained the bones of those persons whose names are inscribed without.'

William was right. They were indeed the names of long-dead abbots. We meet with some of them elsewhere in ancient documents. Bregored was there in the year 658, when the West Saxon king Cenwalh annexed this part of Somerset. As we noted in Chapter 3, the frontier between Saxon and Briton had been held along the line of Selwood for over 100 years, and in that century the Saxons had become Christians. So Glastonbury Abbey was not sacked as it would have been in the old barbarous days. Bregored was confirmed in his position and continued to rule peaceably until his death in 669. Only then was the first English abbot, Beorthwald, appointed. A surviving charter, or a copy of it, records the grant of land at Meare to Abbot Beorthwald in 671.

So, then, we have stepped back in history to a date over 1,300 years ago and we find Glastonbury Abbey a well-established and venerable foundation, its abbot one of a long line stretching back into the mists. It is already steeped in traditions and legends. How much farther back can actual history be taken?

We know the name of one of the abbots not long before Bregored. It was Lademund. Immediately before him, an abbot named Worgret was given five hides of land by the British king of Dumnonia. William of Malmesbury records that he saw the charter and that it was dated 601.

There is a very ancient Welsh triad, of unknown date, which lists:

'The Three Perpetual Choirs of Britain; the choir of Llan Iltud Vawr in Glamorgan, the choir of Ambrosius in Amesbury; and the choir of Glastonbury. In each of these choirs there were 2,400 saints, that is there were a hundred for every hour of the day and night in rotation.'

The numbers of 'saints' may be exaggerated, but the interesting point is that the three choirs are regarded as being co-existent. Well, we know that Amesbury with its abbey was destroyed by the Saxons in 554. Which puts the foundation of Glastonbury back to a considerably earlier date.

The sacking of Amesbury was an episode in the Saxon advance after the death of the British hero, Arthur (see pages 27–31). Leading authorities suggest the year 538 as the date of Arthur's demise. He fell in internecine war at a battle named Camlann. Tradition places this by the little river Cam, in the meadows below Cadbury Camp. Not far from Glastonbury.

With such close juxtaposition we might expect legend to be busy linking Arthur with Glastonbury, and so it has. Causeways may still be traced carrying a road from Cadbury to Glastonbury. Along the line of the road we may still cross an Arthur's Bridge.

According to Tennyson, it was along this track that the mortally wounded Arthur, supported by the last of his knights, Bedivere, staggered towards

> . . . the island valley of Avilion;
> Where falls not hail, or rain, or any snow,
> Nor ever wind blows loudly; but it lies,
> Deep-meadow'd, happy, fair with orchard lawns
> And bowery hollows crowned with summer sea,
> Where I will heal me of my grievous wound.

Avalon. The islands of apples. The mystic land which romance has identified with Glastonbury.

> Then murmur'd Arthur, 'Place me in the barge.'
> So to the barge they came. There those three Queens
> Put forth their hands, and took the King and wept.

So the barge, 'dark as a funeral scarf from stem to stern', moved silently away across the dark waters of the lake towards the magic island, where heroes rest until their country needs them again.

It is, of course, all legend, and yet the tradition persisted throughout the centuries that Arthur was buried at Glastonbury. The Welsh for long contended that Arthur had no grave, for the reason that he had never died and was waiting, in the wings, so to speak, to come again when the time was ripe. Yet when in the year 1190 excavations were conducted at Glastonbury under the direction of King Henry II and the alleged graves of Arthur and his queen Guinevere were uncovered, no Welsh voice was raised to dispute the identification. Because, say scholars, it was widely known that the identification was correct.

Between those two pyramids already mentioned monks digging a grave found, seven feet below the ground, a stone slab inset with a leaden cross. On it they read the inscription, HIC JACET SEPULTUS INCLYTUS REX ARTURUS IN INSULA AVALLONIA. 'Here lies the renowned King Arthur in the Isle of Avalon.'

They sought for more, dug for a further 16 feet and hit the lid of a massive coffin, made from a hollowed oaken log. Inside were the bones of a huge man and a slightly-built woman. The man had ten wounds in his skull. Adhering to the woman's skull were some locks of golden hair, which crumbled into dust when a monk tried to handle them.

Were these really the bones of Arthur and Guinevere? Henry II and the monks of Glastonbury thought so, or behaved as though they did. They announced their find to the world, and no one apparently challenged their statements. The bones were reverently collected, stored in two chests and re-interred in the Abbey. Nearly 100 years later, in 1278, they were brought out for another monarch, King Edward I, to see. For a short time the skeletons were exhibited to the public. Then, in their painted chests, they were carried by the King and Queen to the high altar at Glastonbury and buried again, at a spot now labelled for the edification of visitors. Presumably they were scattered when the abbey was pillaged at the Dissolution.

As for the leaden cross with its inscription, we know that it survived until the eighteenth century, when it was in the possession of a chancellor of the Wells diocese. In 1607 the antiquary, William Camden, made a drawing of it, which is still extant. Experts are divided as to whether it is genuine or not.

The sceptics are doubtful about the whole story. It was, they say, altogether too convenient for certain interested parties. One of these was King Henry II who, having united the whole of Britain,

9   *St Mary Magdalene, Taunton*

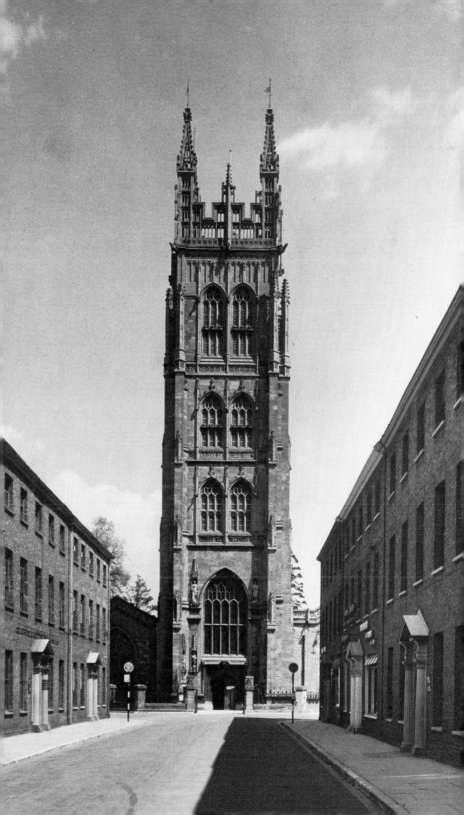

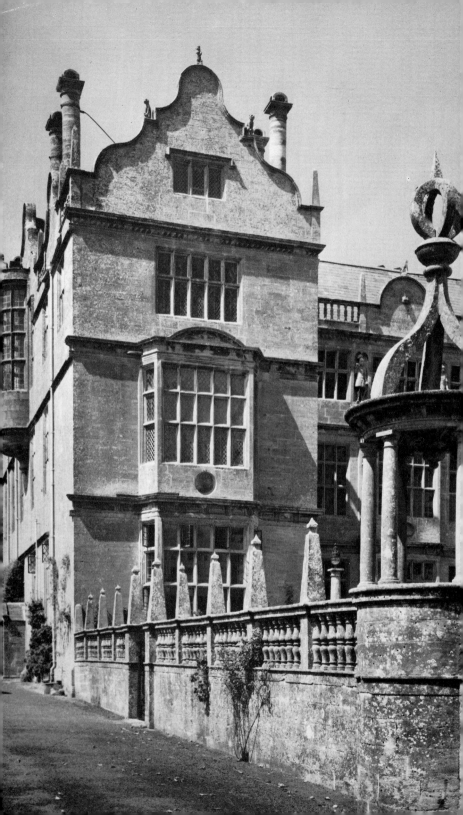

much of Ireland and most of France under his rule, was feeling the need of a *mythos* to catch the imagination of the peoples of his scattered empire and help to weld them together permanently. The developing legends of Arthur and his mythological Knights of the Round Table served admirably. He was also pleased to be able to produce proof to those potential trouble-makers, the Welsh, that their great hero was indeed dead.

The other group with a vested interest in anything that would benefit Glastonbury consisted of the Abbot and the monks. Six years earlier, in 1184, a disastrous fire had destroyed most of the Abbey. Vast sums were needed to rebuild it, and anything in the matter of relics helped. Besides, there was always the smouldering fire of contention between Glastonbury and Canterbury as to which should have precedence. Canterbury based its primacy on the mission of St Augustine, who landed in Kent in 597. But if Arthur was buried at Glastonbury the Abbey must have been in existence at least 50 years earlier.

We have thus already moved deep into antiquity in our search for the origins of Glastonbury. Can we go further?

Yes, we can. Our next historical character to be called to the witness-box is St Patrick. Patrick was born somewhere in western Britain (some think by the Clyde, some in Glamorgan, some in Somerset) between the years A.D. 370 and 390. Captured by Irish pirates and sold as a slave to a chieftain in Ulster, he escaped after a few years of servitude, found his way to Rome and was ordained. Here is what William of Malmesbury, writing around 1125, says of his connections with Glastonbury:

'It is written in the Chronicles, "In the year of our Lord's incarnation 425, St Patrick is ordained to Ireland by Pope Celestine". Also, "In the year 433 Ireland is converted to the faith of Christ by the preaching of St Patrick, accompanied by many miracles. In consequence executing his appointed office with diligence, and in his latter days returning to his own country, he landed in Cornwall, from his altar, which even to this time is held in high veneration by the inhabitants for its sanctity and efficacy in restoring the infirm. Proceeding to Glastonbury, and there becoming monk, and abbat, after some years he paid the debt of nature ..."

'... He lies on the right side of the altar in the old church; indeed the care of posterity has enshrined his body in silver. Hence the

Irish have an ancient usage of frequenting the place to kiss the relics of the patron.'

We are back to the days of Roman Britain. Although the legions went away in about the year 410, all of the western half of the country remained Romano-British and independent for several more centuries. Life went on much the same as ever, though with frequent alarms and raids. When Patrick escaped from slavery in Ulster he was able to find his family still living in the same place as he had left them. In surviving letters of his it is obvious that he regards himself as a Roman citizen.

And when Patrick comes to Glastonbury in his old age, he becomes abbot of an existing monastery. His body is interred in a church which can even then be referred to as 'the old church'. (As likewise King Ina also endowed, in the 8th century, 'the old church'.)

Roman Britain, which we have now reached in search of the origins of Glastonbury, was for the last century before the departure of the legions, nominally Christian. Constantine became the first Emperor to declare his adherence to Christianity. His edict of toleration, granting civil rights to Christians, was dated 313. Only ten years earlier the great persecution of Christians by Diocletian revealed considerable numbers of the faith in Britain, and the names of several martyrs are recorded. In 314 three British bishops, as well as a presbyter and a deacon, are named as attending a Council at Arles. And for the rest of the century British representatives figure frequently in councils of the Church.

So, less than 300 years after the birth of Christ, Christianity was well established in Britain, though sharing the allegiance of the populace with dozens of other religions, from Mithraism to the old Celtic pantheon. Nor is that surprising, for communications were easy in the Roman world, and the Christian message spread rapidly throughout its limits, and beyond, in the first century after Christ.

Where does Glastonbury stand in these early centuries? Perhaps the most significant feature about Glastonbury is that it always seems to be there. Time and again as we trace our steps back through history we encounter characters with associations with Glastonbury, and always it seems a stable and well-established foundation. Nowhere have we come across so far any reference to its beginning.

The monks of Glastonbury itself had no doubts about the origin of their Abbey. In the Middle Ages a bronze plaque attached to a column of the church proclaimed:

'In the year XXXI after the Lord's Passion, twelve holy men, of whom Joseph of Arimathea was the chief, came hither and built the first church of this kingdom, in this place which Christ at this time dedicated to the honour of his Mother and as a place for their burial.'

The story to which this refers is that Joseph of Arimathea, in whose garden tomb Jesus's body was laid after the crucifixion, was a wealthy merchant engaged in trade between the Levant and the West, which included Cornwall. It is said that Cornish miners used to have a song the refrain of which ran,

Joseph was in the tin trade.

In the persecution of Christians which began with the stoning of Stephen (as recorded in the Acts of the Apostles) Joseph fled to Britain. Mediaeval theologians established the date, to their satisfaction, as A.D. 63, though a minority held that it was really A.D. 31.

Anyway, the versions in circulation provided a good deal of detail. Joseph arrived in Somerset with 12 companions, after a journey around the Cornish peninsula. He was welcomed by the local king, named Arviragus, who, although he did not immediately become a Christian, recognized sincere men when he saw them and gave them a grant of land to settle on. The land in question was the island of Glastonbury, or Avalon.

Landing on the island on a winter day and being very tired, Joseph stuck his staff into the ground on Weary-all Hill. After prayer, the staff immediately put forth twigs and blossomed. Such was the origin of the Holy Thorn, which thenceforth always bloomed on Christmas Day, in the dead of winter.

Later they built a little wattle church (on the site of the later Abbey) and dedicated it to St Mary the Virgin. They all lived there till death claimed them. Joseph was eventually buried near the church, according to a fifth-century Welsh bard,

He lies on a two-forked line
Next the south corner of an oratory
Fashioned of wattles

For the adoring of a mighty Virgin
By the aforesaid sphere-betokened
Dwellers in that place, thirteen in all.

Meantime, the kings who succeeded Arviragus had enlarged the grant of land to 'twelve hides'. The Twelve Hides of Glastonbury are a theme which recurs frequently in mediaeval records. A hide is supposed to have been as much as one man with an ox team could cultivate in a year, generally about 120 acres. (By the thirteenth century the Glastonbury domain had expanded to nearly 25,000 acres!)

Joseph brought several invaluable relics with him from Palestine. These included 'two cruets, filled with blood and sweat of the Prophet Jesus', and the cup, or chalice, from which the wine was drunk at the Last Supper. This last was the Holy Grail, which features so prominently in mediaeval romances. The knights of King Arthur's Round Table go out on their quest for the Holy Grail, a mystical experience in which success can only be achieved by the pure in heart. In the romances it was found by the perfect knight, Sir Galahad. On a more mundane level, Glastonbury Abbey held that the Grail was lost in early times, was found at the time of Arthur, and was lost again. Its rediscovery will herald the dawn of an age of peace and enlightenment.

Nor is Joseph of Arimathea the only one of the first generation of Christians who is reputed, by tradition or legend, to have brought Christianity to Britain. Joseph, according to one version, was sent there by St Philip, who preached in Gaul and who may have visited Britain himself. Another story credits St Paul with having brought the gospel to Britain. Another makes the first Christian missionary to Britain the Aristobulus mentioned in Paul's Letter to the Romans.

Gildas, a Roman Briton who wrote about the year 540 and was a contemporary of Arthur, had this to say about those early days:

'Meanwhile these islands, stiff with cold and frost, and in a distant region of the world, remote from the visible sun, received the beams of light, that is the holy precepts of Christ, the true Sun . . . in the latter part, as we know, of the reign of Tiberius Caesar.' Tiberius Caesar died in the year A.D. 37.

Whoever was indeed the first missionary, Glastonbury pinned its faith on Joseph of Arimathea. It is an unexpected choice, unless it is based on some widely accepted fact, for with all those other more celebrated early Christian personages to choose from why should Glastonbury select the somewhat obscure Joseph of Arimathea? William of Malmesbury heard all about Joseph when he visited the Abbey in the 1120s. And yet his is almost the first mention in literature of Joseph in connection with Glastonbury. Was he relying on oral tradition? Were there ancient manuscripts, since destroyed, in the Abbey at that time? We cannot know. But for an oral tradition to survive for a thousand years would not be unparalleled.

Maybe two thousand years is not impossible. For the Glastonbury tradition ventures back even farther. It claims that Christ Himself came to Somerset.

In this version of the story, Joseph of Arimathea is a trader visiting Cornwall and Somerset regularly. He is also the uncle and guardian of the boy Jesus, who on one or more occasions accompanies him on his journeys. On one trip Jesus stayed for some time on the island of Glastonbury, making for himself a little hut of wattles.

This hut became 'the old church', so frequently referred to in early times. For a thousand years 'the old church' was an object of great veneration. It measured 60 feet by 26 feet and was made of wattle daubed with clay. It had three windows along one side and one at the end. When King Ina came to Glastonbury in about the year 700 he found the old church still intact, but reinforced with timber and metal. St David (yet another visitor to Glastonbury) tells much the same story when he was there in about 540. He wanted to dedicate the church to the Virgin Mary, but Christ apeared to David in a dream and advised him against it, on the grounds that He Himself had dedicated it already to His Mother. Later it was encased in a shell of stone.

William of Malmesbury saw it on his visit in the 1120s. He writes:

'This church is certainly the oldest I am acquainted with in England, and from this circumstance derives its name. In it are preserved the mortal remains of many saints, some of whom we shall notice in our progress; nor is any corner of the church destitute of the ashes of the holy. The very floor, inlaid with polished stones, and the sides of the altar, and even the altar itself, above and beneath, are laden with multitudes of relics. Moreover, in the pavement may be remarked on every side stones designedly interlaid in triangles and squares, and sealed with lead, under which if I believe some sacred mystery to be contained, I do no injustice to religion. The antiquity, and the multitude of its saints, have endued the place with so much sanctity, that at night scarcely anyone presumes to keep vigil there, or, during the day, to spit; he who is conscious of pollution shudders throughout his whole frame; no one ever brought hawk nor horse within the confines of the neighbouring cemetery, who did not depart injured, either in them or in himself. Those persons who, about to undergo the ordeal of fire or water, did there put up their petitions, have in every instance that can be recollected, except one, exulted in their escape ...'

The idea that the old church was built by Christ Himself is reinforced, say its protagonists, by a biographer of St Dunstan who, about the year 1000, wrote:

'There is on the confines of western Britain a certain royal island, called in the ancient speech Glastonia, marked out by broad boundaries, girt around with waters rich in fish, in stagnant rivers, fitted for many uses of human futility, but dedicated to the most sacred of deities. In it the earliest neophytes of the Catholic rule, God guiding them, found a church, not built by art of man, they say, but *prepared by God Himself* for the salvation of mankind, which church the heavenly Builder Himself declared—by many miracles and many mysteries of healing—He had consecrated to Himself and to Holy Mary, Mother of God.'

Unfortunately, not so very long after William of Malmesbury's visit, the old Church went up in flames, on 25 May 1184, with the rest of the Abbey.

Yet its memory survived. A placard still marks its site in the Abbey ruins. And Somerset people remember it and the tradition behind it. Within living memory, it is said, the country folk who lived on the top of Mendip would emphasize a statement by adding, 'And that's as sure as Christ came to Priddy!'

The legend was also perpetuated by the mystical poet William Blake, whose hymn, 'And did those feet in ancient times Walk upon England's mountains green', is sung cheerfully every week by countless members of Women's Institutes, few of whom probably understand the allusions.

We have now traced the ecclesiastical story of Glastonbury back, through paths as intricate and tortuous as the waterways which once gave access though the marshlands to the island, to the very beginnings of Christianity. One can hardly penetrate farther than the founder of the faith. Legend, however, has not yet finished with Glastonbury.

Returning to Mendip, let us stand on the escarpment above the city of Wells and gaze southwards (or to be precise, south-south-westwards) over the marshes to the heartland of Somerset. Before us is, as Desmond Hawkins in his excellent book *Avalon and Sedge-moor* aptly describes it, 'an excessively horizontal landscape'. The marshlands are, of course, dead flat, and so are the summits of the hills. There are no great sweeping undulations as, for instance, a little to the east on Salisbury Plain. But, six miles ahead, rising abruptly from the marshes, is one conical hill so symmetrical that it looks like a man-made pyramid. Crowning it now is a tower, the ruined tower of a church dedicated to St Michael. In those far-off days of the first century A.D. there was no such landmark, though hints that the hill was once covered with trees are probably not far off the mark.

A Briton looking down from our Mendip vantage-point at that time would have seen not meadows, villages and orchards but a morass of reeds, rushes and sedges, threaded by meandering creeks, with here and there a broad pool of clear water, reflecting the scudding clouds. By the pools, or on islets in them, the lake people lived. One could see them casting their nets for the abundant fish or setting snares for the wildfowl. The latter would include not only duck, geese, moorhens, herons and bitterns but pelicans and cranes, now long since extinct in these parts but once, apparently, quite plentiful. At night queer lights, the will-o'-the-wisp, would be seen flitting eerily about the marshes, and the air would be filled with weird, frightening sounds.

They were a ghostly place, the marshes—neither land nor water. The Celtic imagination needed only a little of this sort of thing to set it soaring. Life for the early Celt was closely linked with the supernatural. So close was the other world that a Celt would lend money for repayment in the next life. Every grove, every hill, every spring, had its attendant spirit. There were fairies everywhere. They lived in hollow hills (and so had plenty of scope in the Mendips), emerging at night to interfere with human affairs.

The underground world of the fairies and of the dead was the realm of Annwn. Their king is Gwyn ap-Nudd, leader also of the Wild Hunt, which can be seen and heard (by those with sufficient imagination) hurtling across the skies in pursuit of lost souls on nights of storm and thunder.

In our world Gwyn had a palace, albeit an invisible one. And where else would it be but on top of Glastonbury Tor! A Dark Age monk, St Collen, declared that he actually met Gwyn and the fairy host there. Anyway, the Tor was a recognized gateway to the subterranean kingdom of Annwn.

That being so, it was a natural spot for the burial of the dead. No prehistoric cemetery has yet been discovered in the vicinity of Glastonbury, but almost certainly there is one to be located.

The identification of the Tor as the home of Gwyn, king of the fairies, and the entrance to the underworld would doubtless cause it to be held in some veneration. It would be unrealistic not to suppose some shrine or grove on the island, with resident priests or priestesses. In the first century B.C. they would probably be druids.

A speculation which seems to have accumulated a number of adherents recently is that the terraces which seem to spiral around the hill are man-made. We are invited to imagine impressive processions wending their way slowly to the summit. Unfortunately for the theory, half the hills of south-eastern Somerset are similarly terraced.

Then there is the strange conjecture developed by Mrs Katherine Maltwood and first published in 1929. She claims to have discovered, from a careful examination of large-scale maps and aerial photographs, a colossal zodiac delineated by dykes, tracks, hills and other features in the district around Glastonbury. Certainly the figure of Leo looks convincing, and one can see the argument in Libra, Sagittarius, Capricorn and Scorpio, but for some of the others one needs both imagination and faith. The whole map of the heavens, if such it is, covers many square miles. What would be the purpose of undertaking such a stupendous task, especially as the figures could only be identified from the air or a map?

One other feature of Glastonbury deserves mention. To the east of the hill is a long ditch and earthwork called Ponter's Ball. Some have thought this was the landing jetty of the port that once served

Glastonbury. Some have considered it a defensive work, though Dr C. A. R. Radford, an expert on the history of Glastonbury, says that it was not. It was made before the Roman era, and, Dr Radford suggests:

'It is most easily explicable as the Temenos or enclosure of a great pagan Celtic sanctuary. Analogy suggests the focus of this sanctuary, the sacred grove or high place, must be sought near a hill beside a spring. Chalice Well, the principal spring on the island, lies immediately below the highest summit, Glastonbury Tor.'

We may perhaps summarize by concluding that Glastonbury with its Tor was a sacred place, held in high veneration, in pre-Christian days. As happened in so many instances, the Christians took over and adapted to their own faith a mystique which they could not deny or obliterate. Or perhaps they did not want to. Perhaps it is true that Christ Himself came to Somerset and learned much in His sojourn at Glastonbury.

Now, turning aside from the mists and mazes of tradition, legend and conjecture which we have been exploring, let us get back to the solid facts of archaeology and history. Three miles north-west of Glastonbury is the modern village of Meare. A mile or so to the east of that is the smaller village of Godney. Both once lay on the shores of a large lake, known as Meare Pool, the last sections of which were drained about the year 1712. In the sixteenth century Meare Pool is recorded as being about five miles in circumference. In earlier times it must have been larger.

The first excavation of Meare and Godney lake villages were conducted in the 1890s, after the discovery of deposits of bone and pottery in some mounds on the site of the vanished lake. This and subsequent investigations revealed the remains of two remarkable villages, well preserved by the peat.

The villages were built on man-made islands in the lake. Their foundations were huge timbers, held in place by piles driven into the floor of the pool. Each was linked with the mainland by a causeway, which, in the case of Godney, the larger of the two, was 100 feet long. Godney lake village covered about three acres and consisted of 65 huts. These were of wattle and clay, mostly round, and thatched. Plank pathways connected them with each other. The village was surrounded by a stockade, and the causeway, as a defensive measure, stopped short about 12 feet from the mainland shore. The gap was bridged by a drawbridge, guarded by sentries.

The villagers were fishermen, hunters and farmers. Their chief weapons, both for hunting and defence, seem to have been slings, large hoards of terra-cotta sling pellets, which in time of war were heated red-hot, having been discovered. They also cultivated fields and had flocks and herds over on the mainland. They were excellent craftsmen in metal (bronze), pottery, bone, wood and presumably wickerwork. Finds of brooches, beads (including amber ones), rings and other luxury objects indicate quite a high standard of living. The men played dice and indulged in cock-fighting.

These two villages flourished from about 250 B.C. to perhaps about A.D. 50. Their end does not seem to have been violent, though there may have been a surprise raid. More likely they were flooded out, in a series of wet years, a tell-tale deposit of silt having been found.

Anyway, these two villages can be regarded as the ancestors of Glastonbury. Their links with whatever religious community existed on the Glastonbury island must have been close. If Jesus did indeed come to Somerset He must have known the lake villagers. If there ever was a King Arviragus who befriended early Christian missionaries and gave them grants of land on Glastonbury island, he probably lived in one of the lake villages.

The Celtic name for Glastonbury island is, by the way, *Ynis witrin*, which is said to mean, 'the island of glass'. Philologists have supposed a Saxon personage named Glaes to account for 'Glastonbury', but it seems more likely that the name is directly derived from the old Celtic one.

As for the merging of archaeology with history, we know nothing for certain about Glastonbury till the Saxons came here in the campaign of 658. By this time they were Christians, and so, as far as Glastonbury was concerned, their arrival was peaceable. Glastonbury was indeed regarded as a token of the mingling of the two nations, Britons and Saxons. Henceforward Saxon monarchs were lavish in their donations to Glastonbury, and much of the little that we know of Glastonbury's history in those centuries is derived from study of grants made to the abbey.

The first celebrated Saxon prelate associated with Glastonbury was St Aldhelm, whom we met in Chapter 3. He persuaded the Saxon king Ina to build a fine new church almost adjoining the Old Church and to endow it liberally with lands in Somerset. After Aldhelm's death King Ina created a unique status for Glastonbury and its estates. He put them directly under the jurisdiction of the Pope, thus making them entirely independent of any English bishop or archbishop. Here lay the source of the frequent friction in the Middle Ages between the Abbot of Glastonbury and the Bishop of Bath and Wells.

For 200 years Glastonbury trained churchmen who became bishops in England and missionaries to the dark lands of central Europe. Then with the incursions of the Danes came a relapse into barbarism. The West Country was the last corner of England to succumb, but in the early months of 878 the invaders surged through Somerset. Just what happened at Glastonbury we do not know. The Danes were there and presumably sacked the place, burning much of it. But the Old Church survived, for there it was, in after ages. The Danish occupation of the region was, of course, short, for King Alfred's spring campaign in that same year completely turned the tables.

The slow recovery of Glastonbury from this disaster was immeasurably accelerated by the appointment, in 943, of Dunstan as Abbot. This outstanding cleric was the dominant power behind the throne during the reigns of four Saxon monarchs, the greatest of whom was Edgar, who was crowned king of all England at Bath in 973. He built a larger church on the site of Ina's edifice, still leaving the Old Church intact. Glastonbury he regarded as the headquarters of the Benedictine Order in England, and the Benedictines were nothing if not practical. Under Dunstan's energetic direction, the monks improved the Abbey and its precincts, embarked on some ambitious schemes for land drainage and reclamation in the neighbouring marshes, and even established a glass-works within the Abbey grounds. The important mediaeval abbeys of Peterborough, Ely and Thorney were all established by monks from Glastonbury. Dunstan himself in due course became Archbishop of Canterbury and was later canonized.

One of the early Norman abbots, Herlewin, who moved in in 1101, replaced Dunstan's church by a much more splendid building, occupying more or less the same site as the one whose ruins we now see.

Herlewin was Abbot at the time of the visit of William of Malmesbury, our chief source of information about the Abbey's early
history. He was succeeded in 1126 by Henry of Blois, another remarkable churchman who, in intervals of more or less running the
country during the disastrous civil wars of Matilda and Stephen,
managed to fit in some extensive building at Glastonbury, including
a new chapter-house, a new palace for the abbot, and a fine bell
tower.

Virtually everything was swept away in the great fire of 1184.
Under an abbot named Ralph FitzStephen re-building was almost
immediately started, with priority given to the Old Church. On its
site a Lady Chapel, the ruins of which survive, was erected, being
ready for consecration in 1186. Funds were scarce, however, and
the publicity and interest created by the discovery of the grave of
Arthur, in the excavations of 1190, were a godsend. So much so
that some authorities have doubted the authenticity of the whole
affair.

This was an age of new horizons. Western Europe, emerging from
barbarism, had suddenly become aware of more ancient and
sophisticated civilizations in the eastern Mediterranean, as revealed
by the Crusades. At the same time, England was brought right into
the mainstream of European affairs by the marriage of King Henry
II to Eleanor of Aquitaine. Thereafter for a century or two England
and southern France were governed by the same crown, and traffic
between the western counties and the ports on the west coast of
France was considerable. It was, too, the age of the troubadours,
who wandered from castle to castle and from court to court, singing popular songs, like modern pop groups. Among the romances
which were their stock-in-trade they could now include the tales
of Arthur and Guinevere, the knights of the Round Tables and the
quest of the Holy Grail, all with their origins at Glastonbury.
Glastonbury was firmly on the map.

The work of re-building the Abbey was interrupted during the
reign of Richard I, which saw a determined attempt by one Savaric,
Bishop of Bath and Wells, to annexe Glastonbury—an ambition
which he temporarily realized. The former arrangement, however,
was soon restored, and building began again in the 1230s. It continued for the next three centuries, each successive abbot adding
something to enhance the splendour and magnificence of the

Abbey. The work had hardly been completed at the time of the dissolution.

An incident in this period was the destruction of the old chapel of St Michael, on the Tor. No one knows when the original chapel was built, but it was demolished by an earthquake or landslide in 1271. A new one, of which the ruined tower remains as a landmark visible from much of Somerset, was built by Abbot Adam of Sodbury (1323–4). Under the same abbot a Glastonbury monk, Peter Lightfoot, whom we have already noted in Chapter 4, spent much of his life constructing remarkably efficient clocks. The one he made for Glastonbury was destroyed at the Dissolution, but the Wells clock survives, though this may have been built by a pupil of his.

Mediaeval abbots of Glastonbury embarked on ambitious drainage projects in the adjacent marshes, confining the river Parret within reinforced banks, for example, and cutting a connecting channel between the rivers Brue and Axe. They kept Glastonbury open as a port, however, access being by way of the Axe. Apparently quite large ships came in as far as Meare, and smaller craft right to Glastonbury. In addition to vast estates in Somerset, the Abbey held extensive lands in Devon, Cornwall and Wales. As far back as 857 it was given the manor of Braunton, in north Devon, 'for the taking of salmon'.

The end of the fifteenth century saw not only the discovery of America and the Reformation but also the introduction of printing to western Europe. One of the earliest of English books to be printed by Caxton was Malory's *Morte d'Arthur*. The Arthurian legends, and with them Glastonbury, acquired a new popularity. With them Joseph of Arimathea, to whom little attention had been paid in the Middle Ages, moved into the limelight. Abbot Bere, the penultimate Abbot of Glastonbury, was an enthusiastic champion of Joseph. In Joseph's honour he gouged out a crypt beneath the Lady Chapel, which is one of the features of the ruins of Glastonbury. St Joseph's Well, near by, may well have been dug at the same time.

Richard Whiting, last Abbot of Glastonbury, was appointed in 1525. A nominee of Cardinal Wolsey, Whiting was a member of an old West Country family of landed gentry. In character he seems to have been pleasant, conservative, cultivated, peace-loving; a good administrator, and certainly no politician or reformer. In an earlier age his reign would have been a period of tranquil prosperity.

He lived in the wrong times. Wolsey was disgraced. Henry VIII
set on divorcing his queen and marrying Anne Boleyn, broke with
Rome and established the National Church of England. Abbot
Whiting, swept along by the tide, apparently acquiesced, though
with reluctance, in the unfolding revolution. His acquiescence could
not save him. Henry, growing short of cash, appointed a new
minister, Thomas Cromwell, who had promised to make him the
richest monarch in Christendom. This was to be achieved by dis-
solving all the monastic establishments in the realm and attaching
their estates and cash to the Crown.

The process dragged on for several years, as far as Glastonbury
was concerned. The storm began to blow up in 1530, when Henry
first mooted the idea of a divorce, but it was not until 1539 that the
final blow fell. Meantime, the Abbot had been subjected to persistent and deliberate harassment and forced to part with both
landed estates and church treasures.

On 19 September 1539, the king's commissioners arrived at the
Abbey to take over. On 14 November the Abbot, accused of treason
and sundry other unspecified crimes, was condemned to death. The
verdict was a foregone conclusion, for weeks earlier Thomas Cromwell had written a memorandum: 'Item, the Abbot of Glaston to
be tried at Glaston and also executed there with his complices.' On
15 November, Richard Whiting, now an old man, was taken from
Wells, where the court had been held, to Glastonbury. There, bound
flat on a hurdle, he was dragged by a horse to the top of the Tor.
After hanging, his head was cut off and his body hacked into four
pieces. The dismembered parts were displayed at Bath, Wells, Bridgwater and Ilchester respectively.

It is perhaps a little comforting to recall that Thomas Cromwell,
the perpetrator of this atrocity, was himself executed by his fickle
master only eight months later.

Few episodes in the Abbey's long subsequent collapse into dereliction are worth recording. For a time in the sixteenth century some
of its buildings served as a refuge for a colony of Protestant refugees
from Flanders. A hundred years later, at the time of the Monmouth
Rebellion, the Abbot's Kitchen was being used by Quakers as a
meeting-house.

As one of the dwindling relics of Catholic supremacy, the Glastonbury Thorn attracted sightseers. Suspecting the reason for their in-

terest, a fanatical Puritan in the reign of Queen Elizabeth started to cut it down. Says James Howell, a contemporary writer:

'He was well served for his blind zeale, who going to cut downe an ancient white Hawthorne-tree, which because it budded before others might be an occasion of some superstition, had some of the prickles flew into his eye, and made him monocular.'

The task which he left unfinished was completed by another Puritan at the time of the Civil War, but by then cuttings from it had been widely distributed. Many descendants of the original tree still flourish, among them the one at Glastonbury Abbey, which still puts forth its flowers in mid-winter. When the calendar was changed in 1752, occasioning the 'loss' of eleven days, a great crowd of people assembled at Glastonbury to see whether the Thorn would bloom according to the new calendar decreed by Act of Parliament. It didn't.

The Glastonbury Thorn is, it seems, unique in that it can be propagated only by cuttings. The aberration of mid-winter flowering is not one which occurs in ordinary hawthorns. The suggestion has been made that the original Thorn, the ancestor of the sixteenth century one, may have been a sacred tree growing on the site in pre-Christian days. Joseph of Arimathea is not mentioned in connection with it till the year 1714.

In the middle of the eighteenth century Glastonbury enjoyed a brief period of popularity as a spa. A Mr Matthew Chancellor declared that he had been cured of asthma by drinking water from the Chalice Well. A pump room was built, and 10,000 visitors came in the first year. But the spa soon relapsed into obscurity.

After many years as private property, the Abbey and its precincts passed, through purchase by public subscription to the Church of England in 1908. Since then it has been tidied up, protected as far as possible from further dereliction and, of course, opened to the public. Some excavations have been undertaken, but there is undoubtedly scope for much more. Legends of buried treasure and lost underground passages abound.

The Tor belongs to the National Trust. The fifteenth-century George and Pilgrim's Inn, once the Pilgrim's Inn, is still intact and functioning, offering hospitality in rooms with monastic names. Among the many who now flock to Glastonbury as one of the tourist 'sights' of the West Country are sprinklings of twentieth-century mystics, who profess to discover an aura, an arcane atmosphere, here. Flying saucers are expected phenomena around the Tor.

In their impressive book *Mysterious Britain* Janet and Colin Bond include a map of the town and abbey ruins which 'reveals the findings of the researcher John Mitchell. Using the sacred art of gematria, wherein every letter has a corresponding number, forming a link between literature and mathematics, he has probed into the magical formulae that enabled the geomancers of old to build the abbey to the particular dimensions that would cause the structure to become a temple for the interaction of terrestrial and solar energies, as had been Stonehenge and Avebury before. . . . The symbol of the interlocking circles (depicted on the map) is the basic figure of sacred geometry, and is used on the cover of the Chalice Well . . .'

Of the Well the authors say:

'The shaft was constructed of huge blocks of stone by the Druids, so legend has it. Twenty-five thousand gallons of rusty-red chalybeate spring water flow through it every day, and this water is said to have many virtuous properties. . . . Some say that within the depths of the well the Grail lies hidden; its life-giving properties await discovery by the Aquarian phoenix.'

We will leave the last word about this haunted place to Austin Ringwode, last of the monks of Glastonbury, who died in 1587. His death-bed prophecy was:

'The Abbey will one day be repaired and rebuilt for the like worship which has ceased; and then peace and plenty will for a long time abound.'

(above) *Barrington Court* (1520)

12   (below) *Tintinhull House*

6. The Levels

By descending from the Mendips to Glastonbury we have penetrated into the heartland of Somerset. These level lands are something like a walled garden, enclosed on all sides but one. To the north the abrupt scarp of Mendip protects them from the north wind. To the east the tumbled hills leading up to the Selwood watershed are a natural boundary, though the Fosse Way may be considered a more precise, man-made frontier. A continuation of similar hills sweeps right around the southern sector. Across the Taunton gap, through which the river Tone pours, the Quantocks provide the western wall of the garden.

A lowering of the general elevation by only ten or 15 feet would turn the whole of this central region, some 25 miles by 20, into a shallow bay of the Bristol Channel. It would be a bay studded with islands, and with the long ridge of the Polden Hills splitting it roughly in half.

Into this saucer of territory water streams down incessantly from the rim of hills. The Brue, the Cary, the Yeo, the Parrett, the Isle, the Tone and the Axe are some of the principal main channels, each of them with dozens of tributaries. Rainfall is fairly heavy (about 40 inches a year over much of the region, though heavier in the west), and springs abound. The difficulty is that the rivers reach sea level when they are still many miles from the sea.

A river's inclination under such circumstances is to dither, wobbling first one way and then another and finally spreading itself like a counterpane over the meadows and going to sleep. Thus a no-man's-land of mud and water is created—an oozy, amphibious realm requiring a hovercraft to navigate it with any comfort. Tracks raised slightly above the level of the black peat can end with such abruptness that a single false step may land a pedestrian in water deep enough for drowning. Alternatively, a stranger seeking to

13   *Tarr Steps; the ancient clapper bridge over the Barle*

penetrate the maze of channels, even in a shallow-bottomed boat, may soon find his craft stranded on a bar of slimy mud.

In Somerset, as in the Fens of eastern England, the flat, unprotected coast provided an additional complication. The slight natural barriers built up of silt and sand by rivers and tides are easily breached. And the tides of the Somerset coast are truly formidable. The normal rise between low and high tide is about 35 feet, which is said to be the second highest in the world. On many occasions in the past when a high tide has coincided with strong winds the sea has come flooding in over the levels, right up to Glastonbury, till the whole of central Somerset becomes again, briefly, the lagoon it once was.

The story of the levels, therefore, has been one of a war against water. The feckless rivers have needed to be confined to definite bounds and persuaded to convey their water to the sea as expeditiously as possible. Once there, the second part of the problem has been to prevent the sea from delivering it back again.

Fortunately for the exploitation of the marshes, the islands and peninsulas of the Somerset levels are numerous and well distributed. Largest and most important is the peninsula of the Poldens, which, from the Fosse Way near Lydford, thrusts north-westwards through the heart of the lowlands to a point near Bridgwater only five or six miles from the sea. Somerton and Glastonbury each sits on its own island. Chedzoy, Weston Zoyland and Middlezoy occupy the Sowy island—2,000 or so acres of silt on the edge of Sedgemoor. Muchelney means 'big island', though really it is quite small. Wedmore has an extensive, irregularly shaped island between the Axe and the Brue. Langport occupies a pass between the rocky peninsula on which High Ham stands and a narrow peninsula edging in from the south-west and culminating near Curry Rivel. Just across West Sedgemoor Stoke St Gregory occupies the centre of an even narrower peninsula. Numerous other islets, some abrupt and imposing upthrusts of rock and some slight elevations of silt, dot the levels. And, standing sentinel a mile or so inland, about midway between Highbridge and Mendip, Brent Knoll, surmounted by an Iron Age earthwork, gives a superb view of the whole diluvian landscape.

The early history of the Somerset levels is fragmented. Before any reclamation was attempted, each island community must have been very self-contained and self-sufficient. The marshes offered a measure of security as well as isolation. The Dumnonii, who inhabited these parts before the Roman invasion and, of course, provided the bulk of the population in subsequent centuries, seem to have been sea-faring people, and no doubt their highways were nearly all water. Roman civilization itself is not much in evidence west of the Fosse Way, apart from the Mendip mines. There are numerous villas within a few miles of the Fosse, but beyond that, waste.

A conventional derivation of the word 'Somerset'—'summer settlers'—would be quite appropriate. The rivers of the levels, descending from fairly steep hills, have through the centuries brought down considerable deposits of rich mud. In summer, when the streams were low, any land above water level must have been clothed in luxuriant grass, as it is today. The custom of taking the flocks and herds down to the marshy pastures in summer and retreating in winter to loftier ground would be a natural one. And Somerton, one of the most ancient towns in Somerset, would be an obvious site for a permanent settlement.

One odd little fact illuminates the early history of this part of Somerset. As mentioned on page 20, the *Anglo-Saxon Chronicle* for the year 658 reads: 'In this year Cenwalh fought at Penselwood against the Welsh and drove them in flight as far as the Parrett.'

Yet it was not until 733, 75 years later, that the conquest of Somerton is recorded. In the meantime King Ina had been building and endowing his church at Glastonbury and erecting castles as far west as Taunton. Somerton on its island in the marshes must therefore have remained an independent pocket of Celtic culture, long after the mainland had been absorbed into the West Saxon kingdom.

It is perhaps not too difficult to reconstruct the general pattern of events in those distant centuries, when the county of Somerset was just beginning to take shape. With the defeat of the British king, Geraint, many of the Britons must have retreated westwards, beyond the Parrett, leaving the countryside sparsely populated, mostly by peasants. Some, like the men of Somerton, would maintain, without too much difficulty, an independence on their easily defended islands. Others, as in the lowland town of Ilchester, where the Fosse Way crosses the river Yeo, would simply stay put and take what came. It probably meant that they paid their dues to a Saxon instead of a British lord.

However, as the realm settled down, Saxon settlers pushed up from the south and east, occupying vacant lands on the margins of the marshes. We can mark their progress by the names of villages ending in 'ington'. 'Ashington', the village of the Ashings, which was the clan of a man named Ash. 'Hardington', the village of the Hardings. 'White Lackington', the village of the Hwitlacs, which is presumably where my own ancestors came from. 'Limington', the village of the Limings.

A Limington resident once remarked to me: 'And I can tell you, there wasn't much love lost between the people of Limington and Ilchester in the old days.'

Such evidence of traditional rivalry between two adjoining places speaks volumes. One can imagine the Britons of Ilchester gazing with impotent hostility at the Saxon interlopers who had come to live on the little hill just across the marshes.

Gradually the frontiers of Saxondom were pushed westwards until even the British of Cornwall were subdued. But only just over 100 years were allowed for the absorption of Somerset into Wessex before the visitation of a more dangerous and desperate foe, the Danes. And here we arrive at the most glorious and significant episode in the country's history. For, in the crucial year 878, what happened in Somerset saved Wessex, and what happened in Wessex saved western civilization and so determined the course of the history of the world.

The outline of the story is well known. In a sudden eruption of furious energy, the nations of the north spilled out of their fjords and forests and ran amok over all the known world. The Swedes went eastwards and southwards to Constantinople, forming new kingdoms in Russia en route. The Danes and Norsemen took to the sea, in their long ocean-going boats with dragon prows and striped sails. Superb seamen, they crossed the North Sea to Shetland and Orkney and worked their way down the stormy west coast to Ireland. They wrecked the Frankish empire that Charlemagne had founded. They rounded the headland of Gibraltar and went pillaging in the Mediterranean. They colonized Iceland and Greenland and even made regular voyages to the coast of North America.

They were wild savages, in love with adventure. At first they operated as independent boatloads of pirates. Their aim was loot, either in the form of gold, silver and material treasure or in slaves. In its acquisition they were completely ruthless and careless of human life. In raids and battles, their blood-lust aroused, they killed for the joy of it.

Later the free-lances amalgamated under iron war-leaders, creating one of the most formidable fighting-forces the world has ever seen. By 877, the year before the Somerset campaign, the Great Army, or the Host, as contemporary chroniclers called it, had, after ravaging northern France until there was nothing left worth taking, crossed into England and had occupied the greater part of the country. All the northern and eastern Saxon kingdoms had fallen. Wessex alone held out. By now, however, the Northmen were being driven by a different motive. They were settling in the countries they had over-run. Their campaigns were becoming campaigns of permanent conquest.

From 867 onwards the little army of Wessex, led by their king Ethelred, with his brother Alfred as second-in-command, engaged in battle after battle with the invaders. In most of these encounters honours apear to have been shared, with advantage, if any, going chiefly to the Saxons. But the Northmen, checked in one place, simply transferred their attack to another. They surrounded the little kingdom by land and by sea and constantly probed for weak spots. It was a war of attrition.

Moreover the Northmen were as treacherous as they were bold. When they could not obtain what they wanted by fighting they offered negotiations which usually ended in their victims paying huge sums as protection money. Alfred, who had succeeded to the throne of Wessex after his exhausted brother's death in 871, accepted this arrangement on several occasions, in order to give his realm a breathing-space. Both parties knew that the Northmen would keep faith only as long as it suited them.

Eventually, however, Alfred seems to have been caught napping. In January 878, at a season when campaigning was usually at an end, the Northmen mounted a lightning thrust at Chippenham, where Alfred had been keeping Christmas. The blow was almost completely successful. Alfred only just managed to escape; many of his principal subordinates fled overseas; and the Danes marched wherever they would in Wessex.

That should have been the end of the story, but the Northmen reckoned without Alfred's resilience and tenacity. In his extremity he fled to the one corner of his realm which offered any sort of security, the Somerset marshes. There, from January till after Easter, he lived as a refugee on one of the little islands in the swamps, the islet of Athelney. It was even then, says the chronicler, only about two acres in extent, and life was hard for Alfred and his small company there that winter. They were even forced to obtain provisions by raiding their own people. To this period, incidentally, belong the well-known stories of Alfred entering the Danish camp disguised as a minstrel, and of Alfred burning the cakes in the hut of a peasant woman.

The sequel is tersely recorded by the *Anglo-Saxon Chronicle*:

'878. In the seventh week after Easter rode (Alfred) to Egbert's Stone on the east of Selwood. And there came in unto him all the men of Somerset, and the Wiltshire men, and of the Hampshire men such as were yet on this side the water. And right glad they were of him. And the next day he went on thence to Iglea, and next again to Ethandune. And there fought he against the whole host, and put them to flight, and chased them even unto their stronghold; and there he sat fourteen nights. Then did the host give him sureties, with many an oath, that they would leave his kingdom. And they plighted unto him their troth that their king should undergo baptism.'

The last clause of the agreement was fulfilled at Aller, three weeks later. Later,

'The chrism-loosing (of Guthrum, the Danish king), was at Wedmore. And twelve nights abode he with the king; and many a worthy gift gave he to him and his.'

Such are the bald facts of the affair. Identifying the various places mentioned has produced controversy. There can be no doubt about Athelney, Aller and Wedmore (and, incidentally, it is intriguing to find these small Somerset places existing and apparently flourishing 1,100 years ago). Egbert's Stone is said to be a boundary mark on the chalk downs near Brixton Deverill, in Wiltshire. It was, we read, 'east of Selwood'. A nineteenth-century landmark, Alfred's Tower, is suposed to mark the spot but probably does not do so accurately.

In January the Danes were at Chippenham. By taking his army along the western scarp of the chalk hills towards Chippenham, and crossing the Wylye gap near Warminster and Cley Hill (Iglea?), Alfred would come on the second day to the vicinity of Bratton Camp, an old hilltop earthwork. Not far away, down in the valley, is the village of Edington. This, according to the usually accepted theory, is where the battle of Ethandune was fought. Alfred thereafter chased his enemy back to Chippenham, laid siege to the place and accepted its surrender after a fortnight.

There are objections. Chippenham is neither a good place to retreat to nor an easy place to besiege. It is not a natural fortress. The village of Bratton is much nearer the alleged battle site than is Edington—why not 'the battle of Bratton'? And, after defeating the Danes on territory just reclaimed from them, why would Alfred retreat again to Somerset?

The Somerset version of the campaign has much to commend it. It assumes that when Alfred retired to Athelney the Danes knew perfectly well where he was. That being so, they naturally followed him. Like players pursuing an advantage in a game of chess, they moved their army to the most convenient spot from which they could keep an eye on him and waited for the next move.

Now, Athelney lies at the junction of the rivers Parret and Tone, in the heart of the marshland. Pursuing the fleeing king from Chippenham, the route the Danes would naturally take would be along the crest of the Polden Hills, that long narrow peninsula thrust out into the moors. From there they could watch what was happening in Alfred's little stronghold, four miles away across the waste of mud and water.

Another little episode recorded both in the *Anglo-Saxon Chronicle* and by Asser, Alfred's official biographer, throws some light on events. The *Chronicle* says:

'That same winter came Hubba, the brother of Ingvar and Halfdene, with 23 ships unto Devonshire in Wessex. And there was he slain and 840 of his folk with him; and there was taken the war flag which they called the Raven.'

Asser adds further details. The ships, he says, 'sailed forth from the land of Demetia, where they had wintered, after much slaughter of the Christians, unto Devon. And there, while bent on mischief, was he slain with 1,200 more of the king's thanes, before the stronghold of Kynuit—an ill death. For in that same stronghold had many of the king's thanes shut themselves for refuge. But though the heathen saw that the stronghold was unprepared and wholly unfortified, save that it had mere ramps raised, yet tried they not to storm it. For the place is safe by its situation, quite safe from every side except the east, as I have seen myself. They sat down, then, before it, thinking that the folk within must speedily surrender under stress of hunger, and thirst, and siege; for that stronghold hath no water nigh unto it.

'It fell out, however, otherwise. . . . For the Christians . . . stirred up by God, deemed it better by far to conquer or to die. At dawn of day brake they out all suddenly with the dash of a wild boar upon the foemen and overthrew them utterly. Down went the king, down went his men almost all; and but few there were who got off and fled them away to their ships.'

The school of thought that sets the whole campaign in Somerset identifies Kynuit with Combwich, the last village by the tidal reach of the Parret before it flows into the sea. Here was a narrow neck of water crossed in the old days by a ferry and known as Combwich Passage. The reference to Devon is no impediment; everything to the west of the Parret was long held to be in the ancient kingdom of Dumnonia or Devon.

We are invited to imagine, then, that in the headlong flight from Chippenham some of the king's lieutenants took refuge in other marshland islets and strongholds than Athelney. Combwich was one. Meantime, Guthrum, the Danish king, pursuing along the Poldens, found himself thwarted by the amphibious barrier of the moors. Accordingly he called up the Danish fleet, which had been wintering over in Demetia (Pembrokeshire), to see whether they could accomplish by water what he could not by land. The long-boats could at least penetrate up the Parret to near Athelney, if they could get past Combwich.

The defeat of the Danish fleet by Odda and his Saxons at Kynuit was the key to the subsequent campaign.

Asser records that throughout those early months of 878 the king was constantly harrying the Danes, with raids on their positions, which indicates that they were not too far away from Athelney. Doubtless the raids went on, as a diversionary operation, while Alfred himself stole away to the east to collect the new levies at Egbert's Stone. From the downs an ancient track, the Hardway, leads across the Fosse Way directly to the eastern end of the Poldens.

Out at the far end of the Poldens the Danes, still fighting skirmishes with the Saxon patrols and keeping an eye on Athelney, where they imagine Alfred is, are amazed to find a new Saxon army approaching from their rear. The ensuing fight at Edington, about two-thirds along the ridge, is desperate, but the Danes, somewhat demoralized, get the worst of it.

Asser gives some further details of the rout:

'Having after a long and stubborn conflict, by the Divine assistance, gained the victory, he overthrew the pagans with great slaughter, and, striking the fugitives, he pursued them to their fort, and all that he found outside the fort, men and horses and cattle, he cut off, killing the men forthwith. Then with the whole of his army he boldly pitched his camp before the gates of the pagan fortress. And when he had remained there fourteen days, the pagans, overcome by hunger and cold and fear, driven at last to despair, sued for peace. . . .'

With a victorious army cutting off their retreat to the east, and with impassable marshes on either side, the Danes could retreat in only one direction, westwards. Three miles away the Poldens sink down to plain level, and two miles beyond that lies Bridgwater. Was that the fort in which the Danes took refuge?

It could have been, because the place is described as a fortress with gates. Moreover it was sufficiently strong for a fairly large army to hold out for two weeks—which would have been impossible in a waterless hilltop earthwork.

Anyway, the whole concept of a campaign in Somerset makes sense. The various pieces of the jigsaw fit neatly together, and Alfred emerges as a clever strategist who not only outfights but outmanoeuvres his enemy. And when the fighting is over, both Aller and Wedmore are only a few miles away. Alfred is known to have had a palace at Wedmore.

Incidentally, one odd little anomaly in the story has long intrigued me. Both the *Chronicle* and Asser record that Alfred's army, collected at Egbert's Stone, consisted of men of Somerset, Wiltshire and Hampshire. But not Dorset. Dorset is conspicuously omitted. It could not have been ignorance of the geography of Wessex, for Asser was Bishop of Sherborne, which is in Dorset. What, I wonder, happened to the Dorset men?

After this brief hour of glory, central Somerset passed into a pastoral oblivion. Aller, for instance, is not again mentioned in any document till the twelfth century. Alfred founded an abbey at Athelney as thanksgiving for his victory, but, although well endowed and surviving throughout the Middle Ages, it was soon overshadowed by its more illustrious neighbour, Glastonbury. Not a trace of it now remains. Alfred's island refuge is now known as The Mump, at Burrowbridge, and the ruin that crowns its summit is probably not older than the eighteenth century, though it represents a restoration of a much earlier chapel of St Michael.

Nearly 800 years later central Somerset was again the scene of a desperate campaign which could have altered the course of English history. This was the rebellion of James, Duke of Monmouth, which culminated in the battle of Sedgemoor, 1685, widely publicized as the last battle fought on English soil.

James, an illegitimate son of Charles II, landed at Lyme Regis on 11 June of that year. Popular and spoilt, he hoped to cash in on the growing antipathy to the unloveable monarch, James II. He also pinned his hopes to Protestant support, which he thought would result as a reaction to the suspected predilection of James for Catholicism. Hence, he chose the West Country, a stronghold of Protestantism, for the start of his campaign.

He was greeted at first with enthusiasm and was crowned king by the Mayor of Taunton. But on his march towards London he was not joined by contingents of troops supplied by the local gentry, as he had hoped. Artisans, farmers, weavers and other ordinary folk flocked to his standard, but most of the important and influential families of the West Country hung back.

Discouraged, he faltered and turned back. His purpose was, he said, to take Bath and Bristol, but he failed to do so. Three weeks after his triumphal progress had started the Duke was back at Bridgwater, peering through his spy-glass from the tower of St Mary's Church at the approaching vengeance of the king.

Realizing the inevitability of a battle, he rightly judged that his best chance of success lay in a surprise attack. Very early on the morning of July 6, long before daybreak, he attempted that manoeuvre on the marshy moors behind the village of Weston Zoyland, where the royal army was encamped. The move very nearly succeeded. His stealthy advance successfully negotiated passages over two of the 'rhines' or deep drainage ditches that transected the levels, but in the darkness his guides could not find their way across the third and last one, the Bussex Rhine. Then a shot was fired, and the royalist camp was alerted. Monmouth's Somerset men, marooned on the wrong side of the water, were sitting ducks, and as day dawned the battle was lost.

The campaign of vengeance which followed was marked by atrocities which the West Country has never forgotten. First the countryside suffered under the brutalities of Colonel Kirke, a royalist officer who was ruthless in rounding up suspected rebels. Then it was subjected to the visitation of sadistic Judge Jeffreys.

The parish register of Weston Zoyland, in whose lovely church many of the rebels were locked, gives details of the beginning of the royal vengeance:

'The Ingagement began between one and two of the clock in the morning. It continued nearly one hour and a halfe. There was killed upon the spott of the King's souldiers sixteen; ffive of them buried in the church, the rest in the churchyard, and they had all of them Christian buriall. One hundred or more of the King's souldiers wounded; of which wounds many died, of which wee have no certaine account. There was killed of the rebels upon the spott about 300; hanged with us 22, of which 4 weare hanged in gemasses (chains). About 500 prisoners brought into our church, of which there was 79 wounded, and 5 of them died of their wounds in our church.'

After certain acts of summary justice, such as the execution of the 22 outside Weston Zoyland church, the thousand or so prisoners were lodged in various jails in the West Country for the rest of the summer, awaiting the next assizes. The Somerset rebels were confined, it seems, at Bath, at Wells (where St Cuthbert's parish church was pressed into service as a jail) and in the county jail at Ilchester. In the last-named notorious prison they were pushed into the inner ward, where, says Bryan Little in his book *The Monmouth Episode*, 'they hardly had room to lie down; being in irons, they could never remove their clothes, lying mostly on one side and suffering dreadfully in the summer heat'.

Early in September Jeffreys and his associate judges began their western circuit. The two Somerset towns in which Jeffreys sat were Taunton and Wells, the Ilchester prisoners being brought to

Wells either on foot or in carts (if, ill or wounded, they could not walk). Over 500 were tried and condemned in each town, and, seeing that Jeffreys got through the Wells list in a single day, the sort of justice dispensed is obvious. However, it seems likely that many of the rebels were condemned in their absence; their names were on the list, but they themselves had not yet been caught.

Two hundred and thirty-nine of the Somerset consignment were condemned to be executed, but it is not known how many actually suffered. Some escaped, some died of their wounds, some were never captured, and some bought their reprieve. Most Somerset towns, however, witnessed executions, in their market places. The victims were hanged, drawn and quartered. After their bowels had been drawn out and burned, the corpses were decapitated and cut into four quarters. These were boiled in salt (half a bushel of salt allowed for each man) and tarred, for their better preservation. The gruesome relics were then distributed to towns and villages of the West Country, to be stuck on pikes and exhibited for as long as possible. One record suggests that where possible some part of the dismembered body was displayed outside the door of his own house. To take it down was an offence, punishable by confinement in the pillory.

Some others of the rebels were flogged in market towns in their own counties, but by far the greater number of those convicted, including many of those condemned to death, were transported to the West Indies, where they served as slaves in the sugar-cane fields. Their fate varied. Some died on the outward voyage or succumbed to the hard labour in the heat of the plantations. Some secured overseers' posts in the West Indies and did reasonably well. Some served for three years, out of the ten that were the legal requirement, and were then pardoned on the accession of William III. John Coad, who had compounded the crime of rebellion by being also a deserter from the royal army and who only escaped death by using a false identity in the general confusion, returned safely to his home at Stoford, near Yeovil, in December, 1690, to find his family waiting for him. He was one of the lucky ones.

The legal atrocities perpetrated on the shuddering countryside of Somerset were effective for their purpose. When in 1688 another claimant to the English throne arrived in the West Country, the people of Somerset were mostly indifferent. They had seen enough of gallows and tar-pots. William III, however, took the precaution of landing with a large and efficient army to keep him company. And this time the gentry of the West joined him. James II, realizing that the game was up, fled without making a fight of it.

The events of 1685 overshadowed, for the people of Somerset, those of 40 years earlier, when the armies of the Civil War crossed and recrossed their territory. As a matter of fact, although there was considerable activity within the county, none of the decisive battles of the war was fought here.

At the beginning of hostilities, the West was mainly Royalist, with the exception of the weaving towns, such as Taunton, where the Puritans were strong. In an early campaign, in 1643, Sir Ralph Hopton marched up from Cornwall with a remarkably effective little army which took over a number of Roundhead strongholds, though not Taunton. As the campaign became prolonged, however, the Cornish volunteers thought of the work waiting undone back at home, and so the army melted away.

Later Lord Essex passed through on his way to Cornwall, reclaiming territory for the Government forces. On his heels came Charles I with an army, to settle scores with Essex at Lostwithiel.

At the beginning of 1645 Lord Goring with a Royalist army was marching almost wherever he would in the West. One of the few surviving Parliamentarian centres, Taunton, came under close siege. Its investment was maintained, off and on, until early July. During that period the battle of Naseby had taken place, and Cromwell's New Model Army had emerged victorious. That occurred on 14 June, and by 10 July the New Army was in Somerset, fighting it out with Goring at Langport. Goring's army was severely mauled, and what was left of it surrendered at Bridgwater a week or so later. For Somerset the war had ended.

Between the age of Alfred and the warfare of the seventeenth century the levels had been transformed from a waste of marsh and fen to the tamed though frequently waterlogged countryside we see today. Much of the reclamation work was done in mediaeval times by the abbeys, notably those of Glastonbury and Athelney. Of course, there was friction, because, as in the Fens of eastern England, drainage schemes interfered with the livelihood of fishermen and fowlers. Improvement, too, required enclosure, and enclosure eliminated common rights. Mediaeval abbots were, however, tough characters, and by the time of the dissolution of monasteries in the late 1530s most of the work had been accomplished.

In addition to draining the low-lying moors and constructing a network of drains and channels to convey the water to the sea the mediaeval abbeys also maintained an effective sea wall against the tremendous tides of the Bristol Channel. After the Dissolution, maintenance work was neglected, with the inevitable result that severe floods occurred. The worst was in January of 1607, when the sea wall collapsed near Burnham and allowed the sea to penetrate 20 miles inland. Thirty villages were flooded, and there was immense loss of cattle, sheep and property, as well as some loss of life.

A similar flood happened as a result of a great storm in 1703 (see page 61), and minor though quite severe ones occurred in 1811 and on several occasions towards the end of the nineteenth century. I myself saw much of the plain under water in 1929, and, as I now write in February 1974, a surge of floodwater, rising with alarming speed, has inundated the whole region between Yeovil and Bridgwater.

Under such conditions, the cattle and sheep which normally inhabit the river pastures retreat to higher ground. Central Somerset thus becomes the 'summer grazing' which its name seems to imply. Much of it is not a rich countryside. The 'moors' are parcelled out among small farmers, reliant mainly on their dairy herds, which are milked in portable bails there in summer. Some have abandoned agriculture and spend their time cutting peat from their plots. This industry is confined chiefly to the moors on the north side of the Polden Hills, around Wedmore.

Desmond Hawkins, who gives an authoritative account of the peat-cutting industry in his book *Avalon and Sedgemoor*, says that the peat deposits were laid down from a period about five or six thousand years ago to late Roman times. Their commercial exploitation began about 1870, and extraction reached the rate of 63,000 tons a year by 1966. The deposits could be worked out within the next 50 years. Formerly the peat was marketed chiefly for fuel, but the modern demand is for its use in horticulture.

The other speciality of the Somerset levels is willow. 'Withies', as willow rods are called locally, have been used for basketwork and hurdle-work from time immemorial. We remember that the 'old church' at Glastonbury was of wattle.

After the enclosure acts, early in the nineteenth century, land-owners began to plant withy-beds for profit. The crop of willow wands was sold by auction each autumn. The purchasers were generally specialists who would cut the wands and prepare them for use, by boiling and stripping them. The wands would then be sold to basket-makers.

Most of the withies are grown on the other side of the Poldens from the peat moors, and particularly on Sedgemoor. About 500 productive acres remain. This is about a third of the total grown during the boom period of the Second World War, when withies were extensively used for making panniers to hold supplies dropped by parachute. Nowadays much of the crop is used by blind and disabled basket-makers.

In times past fisheries would have been a third important industry of the levels. Extensive fisheries, formerly the property of the Abbot of Glastonbury, survived at Meare Pool till the seventeenth century. The following extract from a twelfth-century survey of the Glastonbury estates testifies to the importance of freshwater fish in the Abbey economy:

'The cellarer has a fishery at Middlezoy of which the lord abbot owns one part and the abbey two parts. At Andredesey, another fishery whence he receives 2,000 eels. At Clewer, a fishery which ought to pay 7,000 eels. At Martinsey, a fishery which ought to pay 7,000 eels. From Northload, 30 salmon at the Assumption of the Holy Mary. From Houndstreet, 10 small salmon at the Nativity.'

Although fishing has ceased to have commercial significance in inland Somerset, angling in the rivers of the levels provides weekend recreation for innumerable fishermen. Numerous angling clubs flourish and engage in competitions. In recent years several trout farms have been established.

Eels are still abundant. Each spring millions of elvers from their birthplace in the western Atlantic swarm up the Parret and its tributaries and are scooped out by the bucketful by any residents who happen to appreciate elver pie, or rather, elver omelette. In late autumn full-grown eels leave their haunts in pools and wells to slip down flooded streams or across waterlogged meadows on moonless nights, on their way back to their oceanic breeding zone.

Of the principal towns of the levels, almost all command important river crossings. There are Bridgwater, near the mouth of the Parret; Langport, where the Parret's valley is narrowest just after the river has been augmented by the waters of the Yeo and the Isle; Glastonbury, by a crossing of the Brue; and Ilchester, clinging to the Fosse as it crosses the Yeo marshes.

The name Bridgwater is a happy example of the English genius for arriving at the right answer by mistake. It is simply a corruption of 'Burgh Walter', the town or borough of Walter, Walter being the Norman knight to whom it was granted after the Conquest. Much more important, however, than eleventh-century Walter was the existence of the bridge over the tidal waters of the Parret. Until recently no other existed for many miles. Anyone wishing to travel by road to Devon and Cornwall from Bristol or the Midlands had to go over Bridgwater bridge, as innumerable frustrated motorists on the A38 learned. The construction of a by-pass and, even more recently, the M5, has been a godsend and has given congested, juddering Bridgwater the relief of comparative peace.

Perhaps the first bridge was built by Lord William Brewer, who held the borough for a long lifetime from 1180 onwards and whose name survives in the village of Isle Brewers. He it was who built Bridgwater Castle, which dominated the town for several hundreds of years, was besieged and taken by Oliver Cromwell and was demolished after the Restoration. An Augustinian hospital which he also founded, and a Grey Friars priory established by his son, have likewise disappeared, but the fine parish church of St Mary's is not much more recent. Built partly of red sandstone, though with a spire of Ham Hill stone, it was begun in 1367 and evidently paid for through the prosperity brought to the town by a settlement of Flemish weavers about 30 years earlier. St Mary's, with its 175-foot spire, dominates Bridgwater, and its interior is as impressive as its exterior. It is replete with magnificent wood carving, notably in the screens, choir-stalls, sedilia and bench-ends. Over the altar is displayed a magnificent painting of the Descent from the Cross, a masterpiece of mysterious origin. It was presented to the church in the reign of George III by a Lord Anne Poulett, who bought it in Plymouth, where he was told that it had been in the cargo of a ship

14   *West Somerset: looking over the village of Oare towards Exmoor*

taken by a pirate. The possession of such an item of loot would no doubt have been an embarrassment to a buccaneer, and Lord Anne Poulett probably picked it up at bargain price. Proliferating theories ascribe it to a French school of painting, to a north Italian school, to Tiepolo, to Murillo and to other distinguished sources but no one knows who the artist was.

Bridgwater's most distinguished citizen was Admiral Blake, who was born here in 1599 and was educated at the Grammar School. He became Admiral of the Fleet under Cromwell, after having gained distinction by his obstinate defence of Taunton against Royalist armies for over a year. For eight years he led the Navy in a series of brilliant campaigns against the Dutch, the Spanish and the pirates of Tunis and Algiers. Some biographers rank him as the greatest English admiral, next to Nelson. Bridgwater has erected a statue to him.

Apart from its church and the remains of a few other mediaeval buildings, Bridgwater is a brick town. Extensive brickworks in the neighbourhood provided a living for many generations of Bridgwater men. Now a cellophane factory has replaced them as the prime employer of labour. Cheeses are no longer sold in Bridgwater market, which was once famous for them, nor do many sea-going vessels tie up in the town's docks. But the town still thrives and is as busy as ever. And, as a minor but gay attraction, Bridgwater's November Carnival, with its elaborately decorated floats on which its carnival clubs work for the greater part of the year, is becoming known nationwide.

Both Langport and Ilchester nowadays are places of little super-ficial distinction. In some respects they are like elderly men who, after an exciting and eventful life, have settled down to a hum-drum retirement in a terraced house. Unfortunately for their peace, each house is too near busy main roads, along which traffic thun-ders every hour of the day and night.

An early Welsh volume, *The Black Book of Carmarthen*, has a reference to a battle fought by Geraint, king of Dumnonia, at a place called Llongborth in the time of Arthur. If the usual identi-fication of 'Llongborth' with Langport is correct, the town was in existence in the sixth century. It was important enough to have a mint under several Saxon monarchs.

Langport perhaps owes its existence to the fact that in early

15   *The staircase at Dunster Castle, home of the Luttrell family since 1376*

times the Parret could be forded here. Later it achieved some prosperity as a port, a role which it sustained until the nineteenth century. In the thirteenth century the Parret was spanned by an imposing stone bridge of nine arches, celebrated as the Great Bow. Langport's main street is called Bow Street, though the bridge was destroyed to make way for river traffic in 1840. Bow Street is remarkable in that all its houses lean backward. Their front walls are built on solid brick foundations but their rear ones on soft ground.

Visitors to Langport are likely to be told that the town's Hanging Chapel is so called because of its connection, rather vague, with the executions of Monmouth's men as ordered by Judge Jeffreys. It is not so. Built in 1353, the chapel was once that of a Merchant Guild; later, the Town Hall. The adjective 'hanging' refers to the fact that it seems to hang in the air, having orginally perched on top of the town gate.

Langport church has an exceptionally fine stained-glass east window. In it, among other saints, we find once again our old friend, Joseph of Arimathea.

Motorists on English roads frequently find themselves crossing or using the Fosse Way. Sections of it are still used as public highways across the Cotswolds, in Lincolnshire and in the West Country, where the main road from Bath to Exeter follows its course for much of the way as far as Ilchester. In the Midlands Leicester and Newark have grown up around it. And Ilchester would seem to be quite as well sited as Leicester to become a great city. Instead, it is an undistinguished little place of just over 1,000 inhabitants.

The Fosse Way was a Roman highway and probably existed in earlier times. Ilchester marks the place not only where the road crosses the levels around the river Yeo but also the former limit of navigation, as well as a shallow spot where the river could be forded. There is also good building stone in the neighbourhood.

Roman Ilchester, known as Lindinis, occupied about 32 acres, and the mediaeval town was apparently about the same size. In the early middle ages it is said by some authorities to have had ten churches; by some sixteen. For centuries it was the county town of Somerset, and it also housed the county gaol. This last fact contributed to the town's final decay, for towards the end of the Middle Ages, when Ilchester was already in decline, it had the burden of supporting all the prisoners in the gaol. Moreover, it had the responsibility of caring for the dependents of prisoners who were hanged, of whom there were considerable numbers.

In the seventeenth century the gaol was so full that many Quakers were imprisoned in a disused Dominican priory, a little farther down the street, where, it seems, confinement did not entail over-much hardship, for, said one of them, 'in the Great Hall there we used to keep our meetings, and a very fine comfortable time we had together. We had also belonging to the Friary a large orchard of about four acres, where we used to walk, and where I had many a solitary, as well as a comfortable, season of retirement by myself.'

One of the chief causes of Ilchester's decline was the Black Death, in the fourteenth century, which probably killed off about half the population. Most of the town's fine mediaeval buildings, including the imposing friary, were, when in a ruinous state, demolished bit by bit to provide stone for other buildings.

All the traditional English calendar customs were kept up at Ilchester until about 100 years ago. Pancake Day, Oakapple Day (or Shig-shag Day, as it was called,) and wassailing the apple-trees, are particularly mentioned. Until the coming of the railways enormous flocks of geese were driven from Devon to London every autumn, to arrive in time for Christmas. They seem to have averaged six or eight miles a day, staying overnight, or for several days, at farms en route. At Ilchester a harness-maker used to make little boots of soft leather for any geese that went lame.

Ilchester's most distinguished son was Roger Bacon, who was born there, it is said (probably incorrectly) in a house which still stands, about the year 1214. A forerunner of modern science, he is credited with having discovered the principles of the magnifying-glass, the formula for making gunpowder and sundry other matters much ahead of his time.

Many of the other illustrious persons whose names are mentioned in connection with Ilchester owe the reference to a temporary residence in the gaol! Quakers naturally loom large in the list. Sheridan, the dramatist, was M.P. for Ilchester (1807–1812), as was Edmund Waller, the poet (in 1624).

Ilchester's one surviving church, St Mary Major, dates from the early thirteenth century. It has a squat, octagonal tower and a half-obliterated wall painting. Of the other churches no trace remains.

The sturdily built town hall displays the head-piece of a thirteenth-century mace and sundry other relics of Ilchester's past importance. A seventeenth-century market cross, just outside the town hall in the market place, is surmounted by a sundial. But the weekly market, which once filled the town with cattle and sheep every Wednesday, has long since been discontinued, as has the August fair.

Somerton is another of those pleasant little Somerset towns whose turbulent days of glory are behind it. Plaques at its approaches announce proudly that it was 'the ancient capital of Wessex', but that was back in the days of King Ina (689–726), and nothing visible remains of that period. Around the little market square, with its handsome market cross, are stone-built houses of the sixteenth, seventeenth, eighteenth and nineteenth centuries, and the church, too, is an amalgam of the work of many centuries. Each age, however, seems to have contributed its best, and its crowning glory is the magnificent fourteenth-century roof of the nave, made, it is said, by carpenters at Muchelney Abbey.

Somerton's site, on high ground overlooking the moors on either side, made it ideal for early settlement, and remains of the Roman period abound. In more recent times, in the nineteenth century, the town developed a flourishing cucumber-growing industry, based on animal manure brought up from the levels on the backs of donkeys.

One of the most populous towns in these parts, Street is overshadowed by its proximity to Glastonbury. Nevertheless it is itself of respectable antiquity, deriving its name from the Roman road, or street, by which it stands. On the signs at the approaches to the town is depicted an ichthyosaurus, a skeleton of which was once disinterred from a lias quarry near by.

Street's present prosperity rests largely on the shoe and clothing factories of two Quaker families, the Clarks and the Morlands. Both were based on local products, the founder of Morlands doing the rounds of the neighbouring farms with his horse and cart, in search of sheep skins. Supplies now come from more distant sources, many of them overseas, but the factories flourish.

One of the members of the Clark family—John Clark, who was born in 1785 and so came into the business after it was well established—turned his mechanical ingenuity to inventing a prototype mechanical brain, for the purpose of making, above all things,

Latin hexameters! Not only did the machine work but it still exists, in the excellent museum attached to the factory at Street. It churned out, and can still produce, Latin poetry which scans and is capable of being translated into intelligible English sentences. Exhibited in London in 1845, it attracted a sufficient number of visitors at a shilling a time for John Clark to buy himself a house with the proceeds. When asked what earthly use it could be, John Clark gave a masterly answer:

'Every new thing is an intellectual accession, and every accession may, possibly, be of important use.'

The development of modern electronic computers would seem to vindicate that statement of principle.

A list of villages and small towns of the Somerset levels comprises around 50 names, give or take a dozen or so. I doubt whether any group of villages of similar size and number anywhere in England could produce so much of interest. One reason for this is the comparative isolation of these moorland settlements, which caused each to develop independently and so to carve out its own history and individuality. Another is the abundance of excellent building stone. Good stone is to be gained almost everywhere for the digging. Much of it is blue lias, but the best is the wonderful golden stone quarried at Ham Hill (see page 135). The easy availability of such stone has made each central Somerset village an architectural treasure-house. Not only the churches and manor houses but the farms, farm buildings and cottages have considerable architectural merit. Space forbids an exhaustive survey of all they have to offer, but let us look at a selection, beginning in the Vale of Avalon.

Wedmore on its island almost ranks as a town. It is a secretive place, of high walls and furtive lanes but the usual fine stone houses. The fifteenth-century church has a mural of St Christopher, the patron saint of fords and river crossings, which seems appropriate enough for a place frequently isolated by floods. Alfred's palace, in which he presumably signed his peace treaty with the Danes, is thought to have been up the hill a little way from Wedmore, at Mudgeley.

On the Poldens the towering column which is a landmark for many miles is the Hood Monument, commemorating Admiral Hood, who distinguished himself in wars against the French and who died in 1814. The family home was Butleigh, near by. Much of the crest of the hills here and a little farther to the west belongs to the National Trust and, commanding as it does splendid views over the moors, is much frequented by walkers and picnickers in summer.

Ivythorne, under the hill, has a fifteenth-century house which was once the home of an abbot of Glastonbury.

Shapwick has a fourteenth-century church, which has been little spoilt, and a fine seventeenth-century manor house. There are interesting churches, too, in the Polden villages of Cossington, Bawdrip, Greinton and Stawell. Sites of Roman villas stud these hills, and on the isolated Dundon Hill, which rises from the levels just south of the Poldens, is an Iron Age camp, its walls still in better condition than most.

To the east, where the Fosse Way skirts the levels, traversing slightly higher and undulating land, the quarries of Keinton Mandeville are the source of much of the blue lias stone to be seen in buildings in central Somerset. In this village Sir Henry Irving, the actor, was born. Near by, in the parish of Charlton Mackrell, the mediaeval manor house of Lytes Cary is now National Trust property. For over five hundred years it was the home of the Lyte family, whose best-known member was the Elizabethan Sir Henry Lyte who wrote the standard work on horticulture in those days. The chapel dates to the fourteenth century, as does the church at Charlton Adam, just down the road.

Of the former islands of Sedgemoor, on the south side of the Poldens, Weston Zoyland, the church which played so prominent a part in the Monmouth episode, is worth a visit for its own sake. Its 100-foot tower, with delicate stone carving, dominates the moors, and, inside, the nave roof is one of the finest in this county of splendid church roofs. The tower was built on the instructions of Abbot Bere of Glastonbury in the fifteenth century.

Middlezoy, a few miles to the south-east, likewise has an inspiring church tower which soars above the marshes, and the churches of Chedzoy and Othery, neighbouring villages, though less spectacular are likewise mediaeval and have a wealth of architectural interest.

On the other side of Sedgemoor, at Stoke St Gregory and North Curry we are in the heart of the withy-growing country of the

Somerset levels. Both have impressive churches incorporating work of various mediaeval dates. North Curry's church, its earliest features dating from at least the thirteenth century, has at times claimed the title 'The Cathedral of the Moors', and indeed it is large enough for the status. Among its treasures is a remarkable wooden chest, alleged to date from about 1200, with a lid so heavy that a man can hardly lift it.

North Newton, a few miles to the west, on the other side of the river Tone, although it possesses a fine Stuart church with some excellent wood carving, has as its chief distinction the finding here, in 1693, of the treasure known as Alfred's Jewel. Of gold and enamel and depicting the head of a boar, it bears the inscription, 'Alfred had me made', or, in the original Anglo-Saxon, 'Alfred Mec Haht Gewyrcan'. It is now housed in the Ashmolean Museum, and there is no doubt about its authenticity. Someone picked it up out of the mud when an old house was being demolished.

Back at Langport we come to another magnificent church at Huish Episcopi, which has developed into a suburb of Langport. The stone tracery of its tower is some of the finest in Somerset.

Near by is the hamlet of Muchelney ('big island'), which was once one of the most important places on the levels. A Benedictine abbey founded on the island, which is really quite small, in 939, perhaps on the site of an even earlier church, developed into one of the great ecclesiastical establishments of the Middle Ages. Unlike its greater neighbour, Glastonbury, Muchelney was not subjected to almost immediate spoliation after the Dissolution. In the succeeding centuries, however, it gradually sank into dereliction, largely through neglect, though some stone robbing occurred. The priest's house survives almost intact, the church contains much material salvaged from the Abbey, as do most of the cottages, and the entire little village is dominated by the Abbey ruins.

We come now to a series of villages with magnificent churches, far superior to most village churches in other parts of England. Kingsbury Episcopi has one of those typically Somerset towers, beautifully proportioned and decorated with fine carvings, that soars to a height of over 100 feet above the moors. Long Sutton's church has a similar tower, as well as one of those splendid timber roofs in which Somerset specializes. Its furnishings are richly carved, and someone has not been afraid to use bright paint in the interior. Long Sutton also has a handsome Friends' Meeting House, dating from 1717.

Martock, which qualifies as a town though a small one, is built almost entirely of Ham Hill stone, mellowed to a lovely soft golden tint. Among its wealth of domestic architecture one of the oldest and finest houses, dating in part from the thirteenth century, is the Treasurer's House, recalling the days when the vicar of Martock was Treasurer of Wells Cathedral. The crowning feature of the fifteenth-century church, though not its only attractive feature, is the splendid timber roof, reputed to be the best in Somerset, which is saying a lot. Its 750 carved panels, almost all of them bearing different designs, are supported by great angels with spreading wings.

Continuing south, just off the Fosse Way we come to another of those large Somerset villages which can claim town status, South Petherton. Like Martock, it is built largely of genial Ham Hill stone, but its church, though large and impressive, is not quite in the same class as Martock's. King Ina of Wessex is supposed to have had a palace at South Petherton in the eighth century, but the building which now bears the name King Ina's Palace is not it. That building is a fine fifteenth-century manor house, probably built by Sir Giles Daubeney, whose memorial brass may be seen in the church.

South Petherton, however, has its origins in times earlier than King Ina's, for at least three Roman villas are known to have existed within a mile or two. Bearing in mind the numerous Roman remains at Ilchester and Somerton, just along the Fosse Way, it would seem that this margin of central Somerset, on the edge of the levels, was pretty intensively settled in Roman times. One of the finest Roman villas in England has been uncovered at Low Ham, a few miles west of Somerton. Its magnificent mosaic floor, depicting the story of Aeneas and Dido, has been reconstructed in the Castle Museum, Taunton.

7. The Southern Borders and Taunton

The floods that come rushing and swirling into the Somerset levels, to spread far and wide, like wriggling amoeba, have their origin in the watershed to the east and south of the county. There the hills tumble about like romping children. The little rivers weave their tortuous way between them, twisting and doubling till no one without a map or local knowledge could hope to determine where each came from or whither it was going.

It appears likely that, like the rivers, the human settlers of Somerset came down from these hills in Saxon times. On page 111 we have imagined how they may have come to Ilchester, and probably the same sort of gradual infiltration occurred all along what is now the Dorset–Somerset border. The towns of this region would therefore originate as frontier settlements. Tradition, according to one version of the story, says that Chard owes its name to Cerdic, founder of the royal line of Wessex and therefore a remote ancestor of Queen Elizabeth II. It is identified, according to this theory, with the Cerdics-ford at which Cerdic defeated the Romano-British in the year 519, though it is fair to state that another school of thought identifies the place with Charford, just south of Salisbury.

In prehistoric times the key to all the eastern sector of this watershed was the formidable fortress of Hamdon Hill, or Ham Hill, as it is more usually called. Newcomers to Somerset experience some confusion over the Hams, for there is another Ham Hill by High Ham and Low Ham, just west of Somerton. So this southern hilltop fort is officially known as Hamdon Hill, though local people almost invariably call it Ham Hill. And this is where Ham Hill stone, the basic material of the region's architecture, comes from.

Hamdon Hill, or Ham Hill, then, is the western end of a ridge that thrusts westwards from Yeovil towards the levels of the river Parret. It commands a wonderful panorama across the meadows and orchards of central Somerset to the distant hills beyond Taunton. Warriors of the Iron Age found it an obvious site for a fortified settlement and built here one of the largest hilltop enclosures in Britain. Circling the outer ramparts means a walk of nearly three miles, and the area enclosed is about 210 acres. Strategically, Hamdon Hill is about midway between Cadbury Castle in the east and Castle Neroche, on the hills above Taunton. Probably it was one of the *oppida* which fell to Vespasian in his campaign in the West Country.

The Romans in turn fortified the hill, an obvious defensive precaution for the Fosse Way down below. The site of a Roman villa has been discovered near the east entrance, and numerous relics of the Roman era have been unearthed. Its fate during the Dark Ages is unknown, but certainly it was occupied again for a time by the Saxons.

The qualities of the grey-gold stone of Ham Hill must have been known to the British tribe which first carved out the fortifications on its summit—a herculean task, incidentally. The Roman ramparts and buildings must have been fairly extensive, and one can imagine how, as happened in most other places, local people robbed them for building stone in the obscure centuries that followed. No one knows just when the pilfering ended and the serious quarrying began, but throughout the Middle Ages generations of quarrymen, living in the villages beneath the hill, were at work there. It is true to say that most of the towns and villages of southern Somerset were dug out of Hamdon Hill.

Quarrying on the hill has long been abandoned, and turf and bushes camouflage the ancient workings. The quarrymen have left almost the entire area inside the ramparts a labyrinth of ridges, ravines, terraces, cliffs and hillocks. On summer week-ends it is often crowded with family parties, picnicking, the children exploring the little secret paths which make it a paradise for the adventurous. The more fearless have in recent years discovered the joys of hurtling down those precipitous slopes in plastic sacks, used as sledges. The tall column on the crest of the hill is, incidentally, a war memorial to men who fell in the 1914–18 war.

No doubt many of the inhabitants of Stoke-sub-Hamdon are

descendants of the folk who once lived on the hill. It is a large village, most of the houses being, naturally, built of Ham Hill stone and many of considerable architectural interest. Its lovely church is basically the original Norman edifice, to which successive generations have added transepts, windows, decorations and tombs. Fourteenth-century Stoke-sub-Hamdon Priory is now National Trust property. Its great hall, which is open to the public, was part of the residence of the priests who served the chantry of St Nicholas.

Moving along the ridge from Hamdon Hill towards Yeovil, two rather abrupt and conical hills look as though they were made for fortification, and it is no surprise to learn that the Normans built a castle on one of them. It was run up quickly, soon after the Conquest, by Robert de Mortain, who had been granted the manor, and was attacked, though fruitlessly, by the outraged local Saxons, who did not relish the idea of this 'vulture's nest' in their midst. No trace of the castle now remains. Nor do earlier ages seem to have paid much attention to the hills as a military asset.

Montacute Priory, at one time a possession of the Abbey of Athelney, dominated the local scene throughout the Middle Ages. At the Dissolution it passed into the hands of a local resident and, through him, to the Phelips family. The Priory itself soon disappeared, and today only its gatehouse remains. It was succeeded, however, by the magnificent Elizabethan mansion, erected by Thomas Phelips and his son Sir Edward, which has been the home of the Phelips family until, in 1931, it was given to the National Trust. Open daily to the public during the summer months, Montacute House is a treasure-store of furnishings, tapestries and pictures and has a superb setting of formal gardens laid out in the nineteenth century.

Montacute village is an embryo town which has never developed. It has as its centre a very attractive square, from which streets of handsome stone houses lead off in various directions, but, happily, they lead only to meadows and woods. The dedication to St Michael would lead one to suspect that the tower on the hill above Montacute, where once the castle stood, would be of considerable antiquity and interest, but it is not. It was erected only in 1760, as a prospect tower or folly.

Moving eastwards along the ridge, we come to Yeovil, one of the busiest and most forward-looking of Somerset towns. In addition to its gloving factories, a traditional industry, it is the home of Westland aircraft, now specializing in helicopters, who have their own private airfield on the outskirts. Yeovil, in spite of these thriving activities, is primarily a market town, with two weekly agricultural markets, on Mondays and Fridays. Fridays and Saturdays are also shopping days, when villagers pouring in by bus and car squeeze into the shops till the latter almost burst at the seams.

Yeovil began its career in Roman days. Apparently soon after the Roman conquest the legions metalled a secondary road from Ilchester to Dorchester, and a settlement grew up around a Roman villa the foundations of which have been excavated by Westland Road. In the dark centuries which followed the withdrawal of the legions, it is likely that any survivors left the Yeovil site for the comparatively safer walled town of Ilchester.

The name 'Yeovil' is given as *'Ġifle'* in the earliest Saxon charter which mentions it. *Ġifle* is pronounced *Yivel* and means 'a river'. However, the 'v' is capable of transposition into a 'w'. The numerous mediaeval variations in spelling, such as *Ġivle*, *Yevele*, *Yeavele* and *Jyvele*, were thus all pronounced either *Yevell* or *Yewell*, with the accent on the first syllable. The river was also known by the same name, and the town on the river, a little farther downstream, was *Ivelchester*, or Ilchester (which old inhabitants always pronounced *Yelchester* or something like it—never Ilchester). Yeovil and Ilchester are therefore demonstrated to be basically the same name.

To mark the centenary of the modern Corporation of Yeovil in 1954, the mayor, aldermen and burgesses published an admirable little book, compiled by an old friend of mine, Mr John Goodchild, who was editor of the *Western Gazette* from 1922 to 1951, on the history of the town. Though filled with fascinating detail for anyone with an interest in local history, it underlines the fact that most of the great events of national history by-passed the town more effectively than the present main-road system does. There was an inconclusive fight by Babylon Hill between Royalists and Parliamentarians in 1642, and eight Yeovil men are said to have been executed for their part in the Monmouth Rebellion. But in general Yeovil was one of those happy places where little of overwhelming importance ever happened.

Yeovil's handsome parish church, of St John the Baptist, was built in the Perpendicular style between 1380 and 1400, since when it has been little altered. It therefore has the unusual distinction of being a pure example of one style, and the masterly design allows so much space to windows that the church is often called 'The Lantern of the West'. Almost needless to say, the church is built of mellowed Ham Hill stone, as are most of the remaining older houses in the town (though many have been demolished in recent years to clear the way for by-passes and car parks). The modern suburbs of the town, however, are, inappropriately, nearly all of brick.

From its centre Yeovil has extended its limits up the hill on its northern flank to the Hundred Stone, presumably a stone which marked the boundary of parish and hundred in old times, from which vantage point a superb view over the plain to the Mendips and Glastonbury may be enjoyed. This is the view that the Saxon immigrants must have pondered as they travelled up from Dorset, looking for sites for settlement. Down by the river Yeo, towards Ilchester, they founded Mudford, then Ashington, Limington, Yeovilton and half a dozen other villages. Each was originally built on land with a slight elevation above flood level. Most of them now have mediaeval churches, Mudford's and Yeovilton's being fifteenth century, but Limington's and Chilthorne Domer's a hundred or so years earlier.

In Limington church, under the belfry by the great unhung bells, is a curiously worded inscription as follows:

'Near this Monument lies buried, in the hopes of a joyful Resurrection, the body of Elizabeth, the younger daughter of Mr Edward Beaton, gentleman, who departed this life, in the 16th year of her age, about 18 weeks and 5 days before the decease of her Brother, Edward, on the 12th of November, about 14 days before the great hurricane. In the year of our Lord 1703.'

One gathers that it was Edward who died on the 12th of November, but how odd that the date of Elizabeth's decease should be reckoned back from his and that his should be calculated from the date of the 'great hurricane'. This is the storm that blew down a chimney stack which, falling, killed the Bishop of Bath and Wells in his bed. Daniel Defoe, who was writing at the time, considered it was the most violent gale ever recorded in England. It was the climax to a whole series of gales and lasted for about six days.

People were afraid to go out of doors and afraid to go to bed. Many barns, houses and trees were blown down, and it is said that 8,000 persons lost their lives in the resultant floods. Eddystone lighthouse was washed away, and 12 warships were sunk off the coast.

In all of these lowland villages, stone houses, stone cottages, stone precinct walls and even stone paving are the order. There is a wealth of attractive domestic architecture, though the blue lias stone of Keinton Mandeville is, in the humbler edifices, more in evidence than the golden oolite of Hamdon Hill. The National Trust has another property here, in Tintinhull House, a beautiful little building dating from about 1700 and set in four acres of garden and park.

A large slice of the countryside in these parts has been drastically changed during the present century by the establishment of the big airfield of the Fleet Air Arm (it is known as H.M.S. Heron) at Yeovilton. Here too is a growing museum of the older types of aircraft, particularly some of those which fought in the two World Wars.

Returning to Yeovil, the home of that superlative Wessex newspaper the *Western Gazette* which, founded in 1736, still keeps country households in Somerset, Dorset, Wiltshire, Hampshire, west Berkshire and east Devon in touch with their local news, we find that we are right on the Dorset border, which pushes against the eastern fringes of the town. Beyond lies Sherborne, through which it is imperative to pass to reach that little salient of Somerset which holds Milborne Port. Milborne was once a town—an ancient borough, in fact—which has now shrunk to the status of a village. In mediaeval times and right down to the passing of the Reform Act, it returned two members to Parliament. Now it is a pleasant stone village on the A30, with an old Guildhall and a church which is partly Norman to remind it of its past distinctions.

In the same corner of the county, where the county boundary zigzags like a frightened hare, so that one never knows whether one is in Dorset or Somerset, are several attractive villages, among them Templecombe and Henstridge. Templecombe is more widely known than its size warrants because here the main railway line from London to Exeter crosses the main line from Bath to Bournemouth, so the name of the station is familiar to two sets of travellers by rail. It owes the name, by the way, to the fact that in the Middle

Ages the Knights Templar had a chapel here. Henstridge has a hostelry on the A30 road, the Virginia Ash, where Sir Walter Raleigh is said to have been dowsed by a bucket of water, thrown over him by a servant who thought that the smoke from his pipe indicated that he was about to go up in flames. The inn sign depicts this early benefactor of the tobacco companies.

On the other side of Yeovil, just off the main road which leads to Crewkerne, the next town on these southern marches, are two villages with associations with other notable travellers. William Dampier, one of the first Englishmen to set eyes on Australia (and who has a strait and an archipelago named after him out there) was born at East Coker in 1651, in a thatched house which still stands. He had more adventures than any man could rightfully expect in one lifetime, having circumnavigated the globe, spent two years with buccaneers in the Caribbean, been marooned on a desert island, been shipwrecked on Ascension Island, and written a best-selling adventure book, *Voyage Round the World*. In spite of, or perhaps because of, all this, he lived to be 100 years old, according to his brass in East Coker church.

The other Somerset lad with a wanderlust was Tom Coryate, who lived 100 years before William Dampier, at the village of Odcombe. Not being blessed with a ship, Tom did his travelling on his own two feet, tramping all over Europe and eventually hanging his worn-out shoes in Odcombe church while he settled down to write a book about his adventures. He called himself a 'Legge-Stretcher', but his account of his adventures was true and his observations accurate. Impelled to go on his travels again, he plodded on, farther east, to visit Greece, Constantinople, Jerusalem and eventually India, where he had an audience of the Mogul emperor. This time, however, he never came back, dying of dysentery in Surat, India, in 1617.

Yeovil's excellent little library has books about both William Dampier and Tom Coryate.

There are no more delightful villages in all England than those which cluster in the combes and on the hillsides west and south of Yeovil. Here the levels of central Somerset give way to a jumble of little hills, heaped together with about as much order as toy bricks in a child's play-box. They are rich in small scenery. Age-old lanes have cut deep ravines in the soft grey-gold stone, like miniature

Cheddar gorges, and these are arched over, like cathedral naves, by towering trees, while the rocks themselves are half submerged in cascades of trailing ivy, hart's-tongue ferns and pink campion. The villages, well nucleated around their churches, give the impression of having grown rather than of being fabricated. Somerset builders, both past and present, have needed no lessons in how to use the local stone. Farms, cottages and farm buildings, as well as manors and churches, are all beautiful, and virtually every garden is, to some extent, a rockery.

Amid all this loveliness, picking out places for particular mention is a thankless task. Of the two mentioned above, Odcombe is a hill-crest village, while East Coker nestles in a wooded valley, and each may be taken as typical of many others. Some, such as East Coker, have splendid manor houses (which in this instance is mostly Tudor). Brympton D'Evercy, usually commended by guide-books as one of the show-places of the region, has its manor-house (fifteenth century), dower-house, church, stables and gardens arranged in a perfect group. Preston Plucknett, which has become a western suburb of Yeovil, has a superb mediaeval house in Abbey Farm, complete with high-roofed stone barn, 114 feet long.

At Barwick, just south of Yeovil, the park is adorned by four architectural oddities which can set the visitor vainly guessing at their meaning and purpose, for they have none. One is a stone spire or cone which, set on four Gothic arches, rises to a height of 75 feet. Another has a statue of winged Hermes perched on a stone column. All four were early nineteenth-century 'follies', devised to give work to unemployed glove-makers. The benefactor was the local landowner, George Messiter, and the spire, which is gracefully proportioned and quite attractive in its setting, is known as 'Messiter's Cone'. Local fancy has been busy with Hermes. He is known as Jack-the-Treacle-Eater and is said to represent a young man employed by Messiter to carry messages, on foot, between Barwick and London and is alleged to have trained on treacle!

Eight or nine miles west of Yeovil, along the A30, Crewkerne is another stone village but one grown to the stature of a town. It did this long ago, however, for there was at least a church here in the time of King Alfred, and Crewkerne had a mint in the reigns of several Saxon kings. Its name is said to be a blend of Saxon and Celtic—Cruche meaning 'sheltered' in Celtic, and 'aerne' a 'store-

Two Somerset Birds

17   (above) *The Sedge Warbler*
18   (below) *The Hobby*

house' in Saxon.

Crewkerne's prosperity was founded on weaving, an industry which still flourishes. The town, and the villages around it (weaving being originally a cottage industry), was based not on wool but on flax, which was extensively grown in the district. Flax-growing was indeed revived during the Second World War, a mill being established at Lopen, but it has now ceased again. The speciality of the district was sail-cloth, of which vast quantities were required by the Navy in the days of sailing ships. The *Victory* carried sails of Crewkerne canvas at the battle of Trafalgar. Nowadays the mills are producing such goods as canvas for deck-chairs and shop awnings and webbing for parachute harness. The town also has glove- and shirt-making factories and is, of course, a market and shopping centre for the neighbouring villages. Tucked away out of sight behind the main streets a new industrial estate is being developed, with foundries, factories, cash-and-carry stores and sundry other enterprises which make Crewkerne busier than ever. And in somebody's filing cabinet is a scheme for constructing a by-pass for taking the A30 around the outskirts and making the centre of the town a shopping precinct for pedestrians only.

How the annual autumn fair will then exercise its ancient rights seems uncertain. Crewkerne is one of those West Country towns which still holds high carnival on the appointed days. Travelling showmen, with their roundabouts, moon rockets, side-shows, helter-skelters and other attractions traditionally comprising 'all the fun of the fair' descend on Crewkerne on the two statutory days in September, set up their stands in the Square and main streets and disrupt the life of the town. So it has been for a thousand years. The charter granting the right to the Fair was lost over 900 years ago, but the custom is so firmly established that even the iconoclastic twentieth century cannot alter it.

The parish church of St Bartholomew is one of the largest and finest of a group of fifteenth-century churches in these parts. Its style is pure Perpendicular.

The next lap of seven or eight miles along the A30 brings us to Chard, the last town in Somerset before the Great West Road sweeps into Devon. Here is another town of ancient foundation now earning its living largely by cloth-making. Its lay-out, however, is quite different from the cosy labyrinth of Crewkerne's tortuous streets. The motorist tends to remember its broad, wide Fore Street, leading up a long hill, with parking facilities. There is an Old Town, with narrow streets and abrupt corners, but it lies off the main highway. Chard was swept by a disastrous fire in 1577, which perhaps was the cause of its development with more elbow-room than most West Country towns. However, broad, straight Fore Street may mark the line of a Roman road.

Chard was created a borough in the thirteenth century. Its well-known Grammar School was founded in 1671, though the building it occupies was erected in 1583, being first used as a private house. Chard featured in various comings and goings during the Civil War, with Charles I and his army bivouacking here on two occasions, but no fighting occurred. It was also in the thick of the Monmouth Rebellion, and Judge Jeffreys duly exacted vengeance on a dozen or so Chard men, hanging them from an oak which was still standing at the end of the nineteenth century.

On a wall plaque in High Street is an intriguing inscription concerning a Chard worthy, John Stringfellow, who is stated to have been 'the inventor of the aeroplane'. The information is accurate. John Stringfellow did indeed make an aeroplane which would fly, in the year 1847. He exhibited it in London in 1868, when it flew the length of the Crystal Palace, rising several feet above ground. His models are still to be seen in the Science Museum in London, and there is little wrong with their design. However, lacking aviation fuel, Stringfellow relied on methylated spirits, and as soon as the plane picked up enough speed to become airborne, the rush of air blew the flame out! So the old man earned nothing but ridicule, for attempting to do what learned men had conclusively proved was impossible, and he died before his ideas were vindicated.

Another Chard man, James Gillingham, switched from cobbling to become a pioneer in designing and making artificial limbs. Chard today has a wide range of manufactures, from brushes and cloth to lead pencils.

Four miles north of Chard another little clothing and market town, Ilminster, tries to turn its back on the incessant traffic which nowadays thunders past on the A303. Fortunately, this highway, which now carries more traffic between London and the West than does the A30, skirts the suburbs and does not plunge down into the old town. The dominant feature of Ilminster is its church, or minster, from which it takes its name. Ilminster is the minster on the river Isle, a tributary of the Parret, which also lends its name to the villages of Isle Brewers, Isle Abbots and Ilton.

The great parish church of St Mary has the proportions of a cathedral. Fifteenth-century Somerset masons exercised their skill on its exterior in the familiar lavish manner, though the interior is somewhat plain, the nave having been depreciated by unimaginative restoration in the early nineteenth century. Impressive brasses keep alive the memory of Nicholas Wadham and his wife Dorothy, seventeenth-century founders of Wadham College, Oxford. Until the Dissolution, Ilminster belonged to the abbey of Muchelney, away to the north, over the marshes.

The old grammar school, founded in 1586, is now for girls only, the boys having moved elsewhere. A plaque on the George hotel, an old coaching inn, records that Queen Victoria once slept there but does not mention that she was then a baby of seven months.

Like many West Country towns, Ilminster once had a flourishing lace-making industry and also a flax factory. Its Saturday market still thrives, and on its outskirts a big creamery and cattle-breeding station has been established.

The town and neighbourhood played their tragic part in the Monmouth Rebellion. A mile eastward along the main road from the town is Whitelackington, home of the Speke family, who were among the few gentry who supported the Duke of Monmouth. George Speke, head of the family and an outspoken critic of James II and his policies, threw open his house to Monmouth and his men as they began their optimistic march across the West Country in the June of 1685. A royal garden party was held under a great chestnut tree in the park, and neighbouring Ilminster was festooned with garlands and bunting and its streets lined with cheering crowds as the Duke rode through.

Terrible retribution fell on the Speke family when Judge Jeffreys descended on the West Country. John Speke, the elder son, who had led a troop of retainers in Monmouth's army, escaped by flight overseas. George Speke had to pay a colossal fine, as did his daughter, Lady Jennings, who lived at Burton Pynsent, near Curry Rivel. But the younger son, Charles, who happened to be visiting his parents' house when Monmouth arrived, bore the brunt of Jeffreys' vengeance. 'His family owes a life,' said Jeffreys. 'He shall die for his namesake.' And in due course he was hanged from a great tree in Ilminster market-place.

Dreaming and pastoral though they may appear to be, the villages of this southern-central sector of Somerset are by no means stagnant creeks, isolated from the main tide of national events and markets. Rich dairy farms alternate with orchards and market gardens, the latter being particularly concentrated around Merriott and Lambrook. Cottage industries, such as lace-making, were once widespread, and many of the villages shared Crewkerne's speciality of sail-cloth. The presence of Lopen's flax mill (see page 145) was due to the suitability of the soil, especially around Merriott, for flax-growing.

The river Parret, in ancient times both a highway through and a frontier in central Somerset, rises near North Perrott, some of its tributary brooks being within the county and some just over the border, in Dorset. At various times in the eighteenth and early nineteenth centuries the fairly obvious idea of cutting a canal across a few miles of west Dorset or east Devon to link up with the Parret and so create a short cut from the English Channel to the Bristol Channel came under discussion. A grand scheme was worked out in some detail, the estimated cost even in those days being about £70,000 per mile. Although it was never executed, parts of the course were served by less ambitious canals, and by the middle of the nineteenth century it was possible to take barges through from Bridgwater to Chard.

About the same time (from 1836 to 1878, to be precise) the Parret Navigation Company did much to improve the river for commerce. During its régime the ancient bridge at Langport was demolished to allow the passage of larger ships. Near the confluence of the Parret and the Isle an inland port, Westport, was laid out. Records of the Company enumerate the goods that were carried to and from inland Somerset. They include building stone, cider, flax, willows and wool going out and food, coal and machinery coming in.

As in other parts of England, the advent of the railways spelt the doom of all this river traffic. Much of the massive construction work involved, such as cuttings, locks and wharves, has disappeared or lies in dereliction, and it is curious that the same fate should now be overtaking many of the branch railway lines. During the heyday of waterborne trade, however, much of it was controlled by the firm of Stuckey and Bagehot (two families related by marriage), and Stuckeys became the leading bankers of the West Country, issuing their own bank notes and investing in ocean-going ships, before being finally absorbed by one of what are now known as 'the big four' banks.

As is fitting for such a prosperous region, the villages have a rich heritage of fine churches, as well as mansions and country houses. One of the best known is Hinton House, at Hinton St George, until recently the ancestral home of the Poulett family. Twelfth-century Ford Abbey, easily accessible from Chard and a treasure-house of mediaeval and later architecture and of works of art which include some magnificent tapestries, is just within Dorset, by a stone's-throw.

Barrington Court, three miles north-east of Ilminster and National Trust property, is externally much as its builder, Lord Daubeny, left it in 1520. Burton Pynsent, another great house near Curry Rivel, has largely disappeared, only one wing remaining, but the Burton Pynsent Column, 140 feet high, still rises from its ridge to dominate the marshland. It was erected to the honour of William Pitt the Elder, Earl of Chatham, to whom Sir William Pynsent, an eccentric old lad, gave his estate in admiration.

At Cricket St Thomas, once the home of the Hood family (whose most celebrated member was Admiral Hood, who won naval victories against the French in the late eighteenth century), the mansion and park have now become a wild life park, attractively developed and admirably managed.

The attractions of this delectable corner of the West Country were early appreciated, for Romano-British gentry had numerous villas, corresponding to our country estates, here. Sites have been discovered at Dinnington, Hinton St George, Whitelackington, Seavington and Whitestaunton, and no doubt there are others yet to be disinterred.

Our explorations in southern Somerset have now brought us to the valley of the Tone, the exceedingly fertile Vale of Taunton Deane, and to the county town of Taunton. The river Tone, which joins the Parret at Boroughbridge, is little if at all inferior to the Parret in its volume of water, and its valley, bending westwards, must in early times have offered a convenient route to armies en route to Devon.

We first hear of Taunton in history when King Ina, after defeating the British king of Dumnonia, built a castle (no doubt a timber fort) here in 710. Twelve years later, in 722, the *Anglo-Saxon Chronicle* records: 'This year Queen Ethelburga razed Taunton, which Ina had previously built.'

As Ethelburga was Ina's queen and as, from other surviving evidence, they were apparently on good terms with each other, we must presume either that the Devonians had recaptured the fort or that it had been occupied by Saxon rebels. Anyway, it does illustrate one theme which is recurrent in Taunton's history. While of many of the other places we have been visiting we have to record that events tended to pass them by, that was never true of Taunton. The town was always in the thick of whatever was happening.

A salient fact in the early history of Taunton was that, as soon as the tide of Saxon conquest flowed away westward, the place was given to the Bishops of Winchester, in whose possession it remained for more than a thousand years.

Its allegiance to the bishopric of Winchester accounted for Taunton's peculiar status in Somerset in the Middle Ages. Until now we have been in territory which in mediaeval times belonged to big ecclesiastical establishments based in Somerset, the chief of which were Glastonbury and Wells (frequently at loggerheads with each other), with Muchelney and Athelney as minor luminaries. By them Taunton must have been regarded as representing a somewhat unwelcome alien influence, which may be the reason for the long predominance of Ilchester, a much smaller town, as county town with assizes and the county prison.

The anomaly was temporarily removed in the twelfth century when Henry of Blois (whom we have met earlier, see page 102) was both Abbot of Glastonbury and Bishop of Winchester. He used his position to have built at Taunton a massive Norman keep—Taunton Castle. The keep has now disappeared, but parts of the Castle, more particularly the rambling later additions, remain and now house the splendid county Museum. Henry is the benefactor normally given the credit of founding Taunton Priory, though he may have built on earlier foundations. Slight vestiges of the Priory may still be seen, but the house which now bears the name 'The Priory' is eighteenth-century, though some of the carved stones from the old building are in its garden walls.

During the mediaeval centuries Taunton, under the generally tolerant rule of the bishops of Winchester, developed a flourishing wool trade, and by the fifteenth century it had numerous prosperous wool merchants among its citizens. To the end of that century belongs the imposing church of St Mary Magdalene, with its west tower of red sandstone rising to a height of 163 feet. Just over 100 years ago this tower, on being found to be unsafe, was taken down and rebuilt, stone by stone, exactly as the original.

Perhaps because of the absence of their landlord, the citizens of Taunton acquired a strong spirit of independence which led the town to become in later centuries a stronghold of Puritanism. This almost inevitably resulted in Taunton becoming involved in every current of change and disaffection.

Future and more dramatic events were perhaps foreshadowed by those of 1497, when two insurgent armies passed through Taunton. The first was an army of Cornishmen who were marching to London to protest against taxation. They met their Nemesis in a battle at Blackheath. Only a few months later the better-organized forces of Perkin Warbeck arrived from Exeter. Perkin Warbeck claimed, almost certainly falsely, to be Richard, the second son of Edward IV, who was, according to the version of history generally accepted, one of the little princes murdered in the Tower of London. Perkin was therefore also on his way to London, to claim a crown. At Taunton, however, his courage failed him and, leaving his army to disband, he ran away to seek sanctuary at Beaulieu. On both occasions, Taunton was lucky. Under certain régimes it could have expected sack or massive retribution, but Henry VII, always a monarch to avoid violence if he could get his own way by any other means, allowed the town to go scot free.

In the Civil War of the 1640s Taunton was an island of Puritanism in the Royalist West. The war ebbed and flowed around it, the town changing hands several times, until in 1645 it was invested for a year-long siege. Its defender was the redoubtable Parliamentarian leader, Admiral Robert Blake, whom we have met when visiting Bridgwater (see page 127), who put up a most spirited and tenacious fight. Much of the town was virtually destroyed, but the townsfolk and garrison, enormously outnumbered, held out in the Castle. To this siege belongs the story of the last surviving pig which, to deceive the besiegers into thinking that provisions were still plentiful,

was taken to different points of the walls and there made to squeal
lustily! It is also remembered that the Admiral declared that he
would eat his boots before he would yield. His resolution was justi-
fied, for Taunton was still unconquered when Fairfax, after defeating the Royalists at Langport, marched over to relieve it.

Forty years later, almost to a month, James, Duke of Monmouth,
at the head of his invading army entered Taunton. This was on 18
June 1685, the Duke having landed at Lyme Regis seven days earlier.
It seems that the citizens of Taunton, in spite of their Puritan sympathies and their distrust of James II, greeted him with mixed feel-
ings, for some of Monmouth's officers had to threaten 'to run swords
through the guts' of some of the Corporation before they could be
persuaded to march off to the Market Place to hear Monmouth's
Declaration read. However, though somewhat discouraged by his
patchy reception and by the disturbing lack of support by the local
gentry, on 20 June the Duke of Monmouth was proclaimed King of
England in Taunton.

Next day the army moved on to Bridgwater. The subsequent
course of the disastrous campaign we have already followed to its
final ruin at Sedgmoor. Naturally enough, in the retribution that en-
sued, Taunton again figured prominently. When, on 17 September
1685, Judge Jeffreys and his fellow judges arrived at Taunton he
found 1,811 names on the list of rebel prisoners waiting to be tried,
or rather sentenced. The total is, however, misleading. Only about
500 were actually present. Most of the rest were in hiding, though
some were dead. By the evening of 19 September Jeffreys and his
panel of judges were off again, to Bristol, having sentenced most of
the accused to death. That, however, was only to be expected, seeing that nearly all of them pleaded guilty.

However, the total of those actually executed seems to have been
smaller than is sometimes supposed. King James and his Court had
an eye to the cash value of their captives. Almost all those of noble
birth and/or deep pockets were allowed to purchase their freedom,
at often enormous sums. Most of the others were earmarked for
transportation to the plantations of the West Indies, their cash
value, according to one estimate, being £10 to £15 per head.
Legally, they were to serve as slaves for ten years, after which they
were free again. The nobility of the Court shared them out between
them, the Queen being given a batch of about 1,000. Edmund

Prideaux, of Ford Abbey, whose Puritan sympathies and considerable fortune were well known, was handed over to Jeffreys himself, as his share of the loot. Jeffreys allowed him to ransom himself for the prodigious sum of £14,500, with which Jeffreys purchased a large estate in Leicestershire.

The affair of the 'maids of Taunton' is particularly interesting. On 19 June, the day after the Duke of Monmouth's triumphal entry into Taunton, the girls of the town's select 'young ladies' academy' staged a welcome ceremony for him. Led by their headmistress, Miss Mary Blake, who carried a Bible and a naked sword, the 40 girls, in their Sunday best, trotted through the streets in a gala procession and presented banners to the Duke. One even offered a flag bearing a crown and an inscription, in gold letters, 'J.R.', for 'Jacobus Rex'— King James, which was the title the Duke hoped to take.

Naturally, some punishment was to be expected for this crime. The little girls were presented to the Queen's Maids of Honour, to do as they liked with. Eventually, after prolonged negotiations which must have kept their parents in an agony of suspense, they were ransomed for a sum of between £2,000 and £3,000. The parents, most of them wealthy merchants in Taunton or members of county families in the vicinity, could thus consider that they got off fairly lightly. Miss Blake, arrested and shut up in Dorchester gaol, died there in November. Her colleague, Miss Susanna Musgrave, though unpardoned, was apparently never apprehended.

The executions in Taunton took place on the site of the present Market House—in public, of course. The streets, it is recorded, were crowded with mourners. The family of one victim, Benjamin Hewling, son of a rich merchant, secured the exemption of his body from quartering by payment of a huge sum, £1,000. His body is buried in St Mary Magdalene. Of the survivors of those who were transported, many returned home after a general pardon by William III, in 1691, though some stayed voluntarily in the West Indies.

Local legend has been busy with the hated Judge Jeffreys. When James II fled, Jeffreys tried to follow him but was captured and shut up in the Tower of London, to protect him from lynching. There he died and was buried in April 1689, less than four years after his infamous circuit in the West. It is said that three years later his body was disinterred and reburied in the family vault in the City. But Somerset people think otherwise.

There is another family vault in Somerset, in the little village of Stocklinch Ottersay, near Ilminster, where Jeffreys' sister Mary lived. It is said that she arranged to have the body brought down secretly, in a plain lead coffin, and buried there. Somerset people, however, got wind of what was on and waylaid the coffin. They broke it open, cut off Jeffreys' head and hanged the body on gallows in Taunton Market-place. By night, the body was retrieved and taken by stealth to Stocklinch, where it was placed, in its coffin, in the church vaults. In winter, the vault is often flooded, and then the coffin, leaden though it is, floats, always with its feet towards the entrance steps. The vault was sealed in 1934.

In Taunton itself the ghost of Judge Jeffreys is said to walk on September nights (September being the month of the Bloody Assize) in the Great Hall of Taunton Castle.

After the over-exciting events of the seventeenth century Taunton settled down to its old commercial interests. The making of serge, which for long had been its speciality, was, to some extent, super-seded by silk weaving. Later it became well known for its shirts and collars, a manufacture still carried on on a large scale by the Van Heusen factory. Since Stuart times, Taunton has been largely rebuilt, most of the architecture in the town's centre being Georgian, Victorian or twentieth-century.

Taunton is still a busy market town as well as the administrative centre of Somerset. It also has excellent shopping facilities but, situated as it is on the notorious A38 road, the main artery from the Midlands to the West Country, it has suffered in recent years from massive congestion, to be relieved at last by the extension of the M5 motorway by-passing it.

The Vale of Taunton Deane, claimed to be 'the most fertile of all English valleys', is, to a greater extent even than the Isle of Avalon, the ancient land of apples, a countryside of apple-trees. In May the apple orchards spread a foamy carpet of pink candy-floss over the landscape. In autumn the wind-shaken apples submerge the pastures under a pebbly pavement of green and red, their quantities being so great that they are gathered up by a modern machine which operates on the lines of a giant carpet-sweeper, preparatory to their being conveyed by the truckload to the Taunton Cider Company's factory at Norton Fitzwarren. And at all seasons Somerset men need no excuse to drain a mug of golden cider, the nectar of the West.

Cider-making is a one-time cottage or farmhouse industry that has become big business. Taunton Cider Company, one of the largest of such enterprises in Britain, uses about 18,000 tons of apples a year and expects to increase its capacity to 30,000 tons within the next eight or ten years.

Some of the farmhouse presses still operate, however, squeezing out the amber juice from layers of apples sandwiched between slices of dry straw. They get about seven gallons of juice from two or three hundredweights of apples. The fermenting apple-juice is pretty powerful liquor, and old-time cider-makers used a variety of additives to improve its flavour, confident that it would absorb virtually anything dropped into it. A leg of beef or mutton was a frequent ingredient, and many good cider-makers swore by honey, dates and ginger, with sometimes a horse-shoe thrown in to increase the iron content. The extras were supplied with no niggardly hand, and those experts who maintained that brandy improved the cider would splash in a couple of gallons or so per keg without hesitation.

At the other extreme from the super ciders were the farm workers' draughts, made from the pomace from the first pressing, mixed with water and put through the press a second time. The resultant drink was, of course, weak in alcohol, but when the standard ration for a farm labourer was a gallon a day it needed to be, or he would have been permanently drunk. Farmhouse cider was stored in casks, and draught cider is still obtainable in many Somerset hostelries. Most of the factories' products, however, are bottled nowadays. The surviving coopers who once made the casks now occupy their time in sawing the casks in half, for use as garden tubs, or in making furniture and models from the hard oak.

The other major innovation introduced by the modern cider factory concerns the type of trees. The older Somerset orchards are of standard trees, planted at the rate of about 40 to the acre. Many of these are now very old, gnarled and canker-ridden, and most of them are neglected, for the apple crop has for years been regarded as a by-product of orchard grazing. Now, however, cider apple production has become reasonably profitable again, and acres of new orchards are being planted. The planting programme is now based on bush trees, at the rate of 240 per acre.

At Norton Fitzwarren and at Carhampton, near Bridgwater, the old custom of wassailing the apple-trees is still observed on Old Twelfth Night, which is 16 January. The Taunton Cider Company is largely responsible for maintaining the Norton Fitzwarren event, which I attended in 1974. It was at Monty's Court, the home of Colonel C. T. Mitford-Slade, Lord Lieutenant of Somerset.

First we partook of mulled cider, from cauldrons steaming and simmering in a big marquee. Orange and lemon peel, cloves and spices, ginger, mace, cinnamon and sultanas were among the ingredients thrown into the cider pan. A very genial drink this mulled cider is. It certainly promoted inner warmth on that chilly night and shouted defiance at the storm outside.

In the orchard, over a blazing bonfire, slices of bread were being toasted on farm pitchforks. When ready, the toast was dipped into mugs of cider and eaten.

There was a Wassail Queen, who had to perform the duties which in the old days would have fallen to the lot of the oldest member of the family. Carried aloft on the shoulders of a bevy of hefty Somerset lads, she was taken to the best tree in the orchard. Into the forks of its branches she wedged some of the soaked toast. Then, after taking a drink of cider herself from an earthenware pitcher, she emptied the rest of it over the trunk and roots of the tree.

A venerable brass band, with instruments dating back at least to the time of Queen Victoria, struck up a few chords, and we all lauched into the Wassailing Song. The version we sang ran:

Old Apple Tree, Old Apple Tree,
We wassail thee, and hoping thou wilt bear,
For the Lord doth know where we shall be
Till apples come another year,
For to bear well and to bloom well,
So merry let us be,
Let every man take off his hat and shout to thee,
Old Apple Tree, Old Apple Tree,
To wassail thee and hoping thou wilt bear
Hat-fulls,
Cap-fulls,
Three bushel bag-fulls,
And a little heap under the stairs.

When we had finished and had given three cheers, another group of lads, armed with old firearms which included several muzzle-loading guns, fired a volley through the branches of the tree.

It was, of course, magic, the reasoning being that if the proper ceremonies are observed the apple trees will give a good crop next autumn. The word 'wassail' means 'good health'. We were toasting the god of the apple tree. We offered to him our gifts in kind—cider, and toast soaked in cider and, bobbing about in the mulled cider, some roasted apples. By eating the toast and drinking the cider we sought to convince the tree of our identity with it; our welfare and its well-being were bound up together. Of course, with us it was make-believe. But in the old days the ritual was carried out in earnest, as a family affair. It was, in fact, a kind of sacrament. Every member of the family had to be there, even if it meant getting out of a sick-bed. The firing of the guns, by the way, was to ensure that the spirit of the tree was awake and taking note of what was going on!

Another agricultural speciality of the Taunton district is teazels, the growing of which is a declining industry though still practised, particularly in the valley of the Isle. The teazel heads, with the sharp, springy hooks, are in demand by the Yorkshire woollen mills for 'teazing' cloth. The heads are mounted on a revolving drum of a machine known as a 'teazel-gig' in such a way that as the teazels rotate in one direction they brush against the surface of cloth rotating in the other. The finish they give to the cloth by this combing can be achieved by no other means.

Teazel growing provides an interesting example of a traditional type of partnership between farmer and craftsman. The farmer provides the land, ploughs it and works it down to a good seed-bed. He also provides the implements and mechanical power for subsequent cultivations. The craftsman, the expert teazel-grower, sows, transplants, hoes and generally cares for the plants to harvest-time. Harvesting is also his prerogative, though often the actual work is put out to contract, at piecework rates. Harvesting expenses are usually shared by the farmer and the teazel-man, and the profits are also shared.

Teazels are a two-year crop. Sown on a very fine seed-bed in March, the seeds germinate slowly, and the plants similarly make slow progress throughout the summer, when the main task is to prevent them from being choked with weeds. They are transplanted in October, into land newly ploughed from a straw crop. A small spade, especially made for the work and known as a 'splitter', is used for the transplanting, for teazels produce a long tap-root which has to be severed before lifting the plant from the ground.

The plants flower in mid-July, and harvesting begins in early August. This again is hand-work, the harvesters moving along the ranks, equiped with strong leather gloves and small, moon-shaped knives concealed in their palms. They have to select the heads which are ripe and thus go over the ground several times. The stalks used to be gathered into standard handfuls of 40 and bound with a twisted teazel-stalk. They were then stacked to dry on seven-foot poles, under shady elms or against rough scaffolding in the fields. After about three weeks of drying they were taken into barns, to await the arrival of the buyers.

When I became familiar with teazel-growing in the 1950s many of the largest growers were in the villages of North Curry and Wrantage. Now apparently the headquarters of the industry has shifted to the valley of the Isle. An expert practitioner at Wrantage once told me that his grandfather had introduced the skill to those parts from Gloucestershire. Desmond Hawkins, however, finds that 150 or 200 years ago teazels were cultivated extensively on both the northern and southern slopes of the Mendips. The cultivation of teazels was introduced to England from the Continent about the time of Edward III, and their continued presence in the West Country is a reminder of the days when this was one of the main centres of the weaving industry.

In most of the villages in and around Taunton Deane the church is the chief feature of architectural interest, and for some reason the district seems to have specialized in fine wood-carving, exemplified best in the bench ends in the churches. Some of the best though not the most refined examples are to be found in the thirteenth-century church at Trull, just south of Taunton, though the bench-ends themselves were carved in the fifteenth century. Others may be seen in Cheddon Fitzpaine's church, north of Taunton, and also at Norton Fitzwarren, Hill Farrance, Fitzhead and Halse. Splendid and imposing church edifices serve the parishes of North Curry, Stoke St

Gregory and, in the Ilminster direction, Isle Abbots.

As in the regions nearer Ham Hill, most of the older domestic architecture is all of mellowed stone. Even the cottages have fine mullioned windows and many have thatched roofs. The houses of the landed gentry are in many instances real gems. Two of the most beautiful are Cothay Barton and Greenham Barton (near the village of Thorne St Margaret). Both are almost perfect examples of mediaeval manor houses, from an age when fortifications were at last being recognized as superfluous. Both were built for the Bluett family, who lived there for many centuries. The old Somerset families are tenacious of their hold on their native soil and have become as basic a feature of the Somerset scene as the Ham stone churches and the hedgerow elms. At Curry Mallet the manor house, which replaced the old castle in the sixteenth century, is still the home of the Norman family who came here at the time of the Conquest and gave the village its name, and in West Somerset we shall find, in the next chapter, that a similar continuity exists at Dunster and Quantoxhead.

In the Vale of Taunton Deane to the west of Taunton two small and attractive little towns, Milverton and Wiveliscombe, cater for the shopping needs of the neighbouring villages. Here we are in red sandstone country, and Milverton church, mostly of the fourteenth and fifteenth centuries, is built of that stone. Again, we find it adorned with magnificent bench-ends. I always associate Milverton with wistaria, which frames the handsome Georgian houses of North Street, and with the cobbled footpaths which serve as pavements. Milverton was once an important weaving town.

Wiveliscombe also has a red sandstone church, though rebuilt in the early nineteenth century. The town had its origin in Saxon times and had in the Middle Ages a bishop's palace, used by the Bishop of Bath and Wells when visiting this western division of his diocese.

Four miles or so south of Milverton, but far busier because it lies athwart the A38 high road, is Somerset's Wellington, the town from which the Duke of Wellington took his title. Why he did so has never been fully explained, for he neither lived there nor owned property there, but the town felt duly flattered and so erected to his honour the towering obelisk which crowns a spur of the Blackdown Hills and is known far and wide as the Wellington Memorial.

Wellington was a great weaving centre, with strong Quaker associations. Two or three hundred years ago a Quaker family named Were started to organize the cottage weavers into an integrated industry. The business passed by marriage to the Fox family, who still run a flourishing cloth-making business at Tonedale, a suburb of Wellington, with a satellite factory at Wiveliscombe. In the first half of the nineteenth century the Foxes were one of several firms operating cloth mills in and around Wellington, most of them using water power, until the development of steam engines in the 1840s.

Wellington was on the route of another of those grandiose schemes for linking the Bristol and English Channels by a canal. This one was to extend the existing canal from Bridgwater to Taunton to Wellington, Tiverton and Exeter. The idea was good and might have come to something in the end, if it had not been rendered more or less superfluous by the railways. As it was, the channel was dug through Wellington as far as Tiverton, and only the last lap, to Exeter, remained unfinished. Its building brought a good measure of trade to Wellington in the early years of the nineteenth century.

Wellington now has a healthy share of light engineering works, as well as being a busy shopping town. Like every other place on the A38, however, it is cursed by a superabundance of through traffic and longs for the day when a motorway will by-pass it.

Wellington lies at the foot of the Blackdown Hills, the watershed between the rivers that flow to the Bristol Channel and those which find their destination in the English Channel. The hills, which extend as a lofty plateau with an average elevation of about 800 feet for about nine miles and rise to a highest point of 1,035 feet, also form, for much of their length, the county boundary between Somerset and Devon.

Their well-wooded eastern end, due south of Taunton, is crowned by the earthworks of Castle Neroche, a prehistoric hill fort the early history of which is uncertain. There is evidence of Saxon work there in the mid-eleventh century, not long before the Normans took over. Its subsequent career was short. After the Conquest Count Robert of Mortain, half-brother to William the Conqueror, converted the fort into a typical Norman castle, with a motte, or central mound, surmounted by a timber tower. That and the bailey, or courtyard, were enclosed by deep ditches and by earthworks crowned by timber palisades. The place seems to have been occupied, however, for only about 20 years, after which the Normans moved to a new stronghold at Montacute.

Neroche Forest, which once covered more than 5,000 acres, was a royal chase in Saxon times and continued so under the Norman monarchs who, as elsewhere, tightened the old forest laws for the protection of game. It passed to the Portman family in the fifteenth century and remained with them till 1944, when it was purchased by the Crown Lands' Commission. It is now leased to the Forestry Commission, who have, from a starting point near the earthworks, laid out an attractive nature trail. The Forest still extends over 2,400 acres.

8. The Western Hills

The geography of Somerset broadly resembles, in miniature, that of North America. In the east is a series of hills of moderate elevation. The central region is occupied by great river plains. Rather abruptly, these are penned in by western highlands. Beyond the Mississippi–Missouri rise the Rockies. Beyond the Tone and the Parret are the Quantocks, the Brendons and Exmoor—the Wild West of Somerset. That the story of Lorna Doone should be set in wildest Exmoor, where feud and lawlessness prevailed longer than in most other parts of England, is entirely appropriate.

The western hills occupy about one-third of the county. The three main sectors are neatly divided from each other by verdurous valleys. Easternmost of the three, the Quantocks, form a more or less straight rampart extending from just north of Taunton north-westwards to Watchet, on the Bristol Channel coast.

The Quantocks are a plateau, rising at its highest point to about 1,200 feet. Eastwards, they fall away, in rolling foothills, to merge with the Tone–Parret plain. Westwards their scarp is more abrupt.

They look across the valley to the Brendons, which also form a plateau, though less well defined. The general axis of the Brendons is east and west, so that the main ridge runs parallel to the shores of the Bristol Channel. Outlying islands of hills, such as Haddon Hill on the south and Croydon Hill on the north, act as outer ramparts to the main massif.

The border between the Brendons and Exmoor is marked by the rivers Exe and, north of Exton, Quarme. These run from north to south and so make a neat frontier. Exmoor far exceeds in area both of the other hill ranges. It is a mighty rectangular block of moorland, roughly ten miles from north to south and 20 miles from east to west, rising to 1,564 feet at Dunkery Beacon and intersected by numerous, swift-flowing streams. Two-thirds of Exmoor lie in

Somerset, the other third in Devon.

Although the western hills comprise nearly a third of the total area of Somerset, they house only a small fraction of the population. The hills themselves are almost uninhabited. There are no villages on the Quantocks and only Wheddon Cross on the Brendons, while the few villages of Exmoor are all tucked away in river valleys. The roads go up and over rather than along the tops of the ridges, though ridgeway footpaths and bridle tracks offer most attractive exploration to those who are not confined to cars.

Our survey of the towns and villages of the West has therefore a limited scope, especially as the coastal places are reserved for the next chapter. For convenience, we finished our investigation of the Levels and the southern borders along the line of the Tone and Parret, between Taunton and Bridgwater, so it is there that we will take up the tale and move westwards into the Quantocks.

We have already had many occasions to note that one of the most impressive features of Somerset villages is the splendour of so many of their village churches. North Petherton, a few miles south of Bridgwater, has one of the finest of them all. Its chief glory is its magnificent, highly decorated tower, 120 feet high and dating from the fifteenth century. Petherton was the centre of the mediaeval Forest of Petherton, one of the great forests of Somerset in early times. It extended over the slopes of the Quantocks; a very attractive woodland walk to King's Cliff still gives an idea of what the countryside was like in those days.

Farther north, on the main road leading westwards from Bridgwater, two large villages claim our attention. Cannington is now the home of the Somerset College of Agriculture, a spacious place with fine grounds where Somerset farmers' sons and other students receive their training. It occupies the site of a mediaeval Benedictine nunnery, of which few traces remain. The nuns came back, however, in 1803 and have left, as a remembrance of their second occupation, an imposing domed chapel, now used by the college as a hall of assembly. Cannington was also the home of the Pym family, John Pym, who played a prominent part in the events leading up to the Civil War, having been born at Brymore, near by.

Nether Stowey is best known from its associations with the poets Coleridge and Wordsworth. Samuel Coleridge, living here from 1796 to 1799, wrote the first version of *The Ancient Mariner* at

Nether Stowey. The Wordsworths, William and his sister Dorothy, came to live at Alfoxton Park, three miles away to the west, which they occupied as tenants 'for keeping the house in repair'. Literature owes much to the close friendship between the two families which blossomed here.

Across the meadows towards the shore the village of Stogursey, now a quiet enough place, has had a stirring history. In the twelfth century a bold, bad Norman baron, Fulke de Breauté, created here 'a stronghold of robbers', from which he terrorized the countryside until brought to account by Hubert de Burgh. The village takes its name from the family of de Courci—it was originally 'Stoke Courcy'—one of whom, John, played a leading part in the conquest of Ulster in the twelfth century. The moat and some ruins of the castle may still be seen, and much of the church is Norman work. There was also a Benedictine priory, with allegiance to a parent establishment in Normandy, here.

There are in these parts some fine country houses, among them Enmore Castle, a massive pile erected by an eighteenth-century Earl of Egmont who was at heart and by inclination a feudal baron and who tried to restore, by act of Parliament, the old feudal system to England. Another is Gothelney, a good mediaeval manor house in the parish of Charlinch. Halswell House, near by, is an impressive baroque building of the later Stuart period, its park adorned with an intriguing collection of 'follies'. One of Somerset's biggest heronries is situated here.

Rural roads evolved for practical reasons. They were made because people wanted to get from one place to another. That is why the track along the top of the Quantocks, eight or nine miles of it, has never developed into a real road. The only places it could link are West Quantoxhead on the north with Kingston and a few other scattered villages ten or twelve miles to the south. Potential traffic is decidedly limited. So the ridge is left to modern ramblers, and the roads go over the hills, from Goathurst to Cothelstone, from Nether Stowey to Bicknoller, and so on. Let us hope that the Quantocks stay that way and that proposals to build a motorists' highway along the summit are stoutly resisted. A few car parks, where visitors could leave their vehicles while going a-walking, would however be acceptable. Apart from the superb views, here on the Quantocks we may catch glimpses of the herd of red deer which lurk among the oak woods, and in late summer we may pick the vast harvest of whortleberries that flourish beneath the trees.

Villages on the far side of Quantock, in the valley that links Taunton with Watchet, include Williton, Stogumber, Crowcombe, Lydeard St Lawrence, Combe Florey and Bishop's Lydeard. Perhaps the prettiest of all is Crowcombe, tucked away under the hills and off the main road. It is to some extent dominated by the eighteenth-century Crowcombe Court, built of brick and Ham Hill stone and one of the finest country mansions in Somerset. The manor was the home of the Carews, whose monuments may be seen in the six-teenth-century church, and then the Trollopes. Like so many west Somerset churches, Crowcombe's church has its interest enhanced by some magnificent bench-ends. In the churchyard is a sculptured cross, from the fourteenth century, and a very ancient yew. The village also has a mediaeval church house, once used as a school and also as almshouses but now, I believe, as a parish hall.

Stogumber, a few miles across the valley from Crowcombe, was once famous for its ale, made with the help of a mineral spring in the village. The fine country house of Combe Sydenham, near by, was the home of the Sydenham family, which provided a daughter, Elizabeth, to marry Sir Francis Drake. It is said that Elizabeth, tired of waiting for Sir Francis to come home from sea, decided to marry another man, but was halted on her way to the church by a meteorite which struck the path in front of her. This she took as a sign that Francis was the man for her, and so she waited. The meteorite was afterwards kept as a memento and was known as Drake's Cannon-ball, but where it is now I do not know. Another member of the Sydenham family, Sir George, fought for the king in the Civil War, and his ghost still rides down Sydenham Combe on certain nights.

Cothelstone, near the southern end of the Quantocks, also has a splendid manor house, built in Stuart times. Here we come across another echo of the Monmouth Rebellion, for two of the most im-portant rebels were hanged outside the house, to teach its owner, Lord Stawell, a lesson. Lord Stawell was no sympathizer of Mon-mouth's, but Jeffreys' barbarities in the course of the Bloody Assize so incensed him that he refused to entertain the Judge. So Jeffreys took his revenge in this fashion.

At Cothelstone, too, we meet St Dunstan again. His portrait is in a stained-glass window of the Stawell chapel of Cothelstone's little church, dressed in a yellow gown and with his blacksmith's tongs in his hand. That other Somerset saint, Aldhelm, whom we met in east Somerset, is also depicted there.

Bishop's Lydeard, like most of the villages in this valley, has a church of red sandstone, the local stone, and this is probably the finest of the lot; some say, the best in Somerset, at least in respect of its magnificent tower. It has a fan-vaulted screen and, again like so many west Somerset churches, a wealth of bench-ends carved, with more than a trace of genius, with typical Somerset scenes, including one of a stag.

The rectory of Combe Florey, a village as lovely as its name, just up the road from Bishop's Lydeard, was for about 15 years the home of Sydney Smith, parson, writer and one of the founders of *The Edinburgh Review*. Next village, along the narrow and secret Somerset lanes, is Lydeard St Lawrence, where the Southey family had their home. Perhaps it is no chance that this beautiful zone of Somerset seems to breed poets.

Moving westwards, we find we have to skirt the great rounded massif of the Brendons, which is virtually uninhabited, and search for the villages in secretive valleys between the foothills. All are small, though most have been there for more than a thousand years. Brompton Ralph, one of the larger ones, has another of those lofty towers characteristic of our county. Monksilver (does its name mean 'Monks' Wood'?) has a fine waggon roof to its church. Treborough is one of those names which are a snare for the amateur philologist, for the second element in it has nothing to do with the Saxon word 'borough' but is derived from the Celtic 'berw', a waterfall. And there, behind the village, the waterfall still pours its torrent over a 30-foot cliff.

Lonely and indeed desolate though they are, the Brendon Hills were once, about 100 years ago, the scene of much industrial activity. There is iron ore in the hills. It was exploited, to an unknown extent, in Roman times and later, by German miners, during the Tudor era. Mining on a small scale seems to have continued from that time until the nineteenth century. Two samples of Brendon iron ore were displayed at the Great Exhibition of 1581. Soon afterwards the commercial exploitation of the deposits by a company based at Ebbw Vale, in South Wales, began. The ore was found to be particularly suitable for making Bessemer steel. So a thriving trade soon developed, the ore being taken down to Watchet for shipping across the Channel to Newport. At first horses and carts, hired from farmers, transported it from the mines to the coast, but in 1855 a bill authorizing the construction of a railway was passed by Parliament. The line was planned to lead uphill from Watchet harbour to the crest of the Brendons near Raleigh's Cross and then, possibly, along the watershed westwards. The total length was to be just over 13 miles.

By 1857 the railway had been completed from Watchet to Combe Row, at the foot of the hills, and the harbour had been repaired. Five or six mines were in production, and 1857 saw the export of 9,642 tons of ore to South Wales. By 1859 this total had risen to 23,183, and in the 1860s it was averaging 30,000 tons. In May 1858, the incline which took the railway, by a one-in-four gradient, from Combe Row to the summit of the Brendons, was officially opened, though it seems not to have been fully functional until 1861, when the winding engine, for taking the trains to the top and steadying them on the way down, was finally installed. The abandoned cutting is, naturally, still a feature of the Brendon landscape. It was a prodigious undertaking, and one is not surprised to learn that it cost £82,000, a sum far exceeding the original estimates for the whole railway.

At the zenith of the mining prosperity, in the 1860s, a total of nearly 1,000 men were employed, some 300 or so in actual mining. At first the miners lodged in farms and cottages in the district, but soon a village, which at one time had a population of about 250, sprang up near Raleigh's Cross and was known as Brendon Hill village.

As the village more or less belonged to the mining company, the directors could make what rules they liked, and it seems they were staunch Nonconformists and teetotallers. It was therefore run strictly 'on the total abstinence principle', and self-indulgent miners had to walk half a mile to the inn at Raleigh's Cross for a drink. There free fights broke out from time to time, though not often with serious results. The village had a general stores, a coal depot and a temperance hotel. It had three places of worship, one each for the Church of England (a corrugated iron mission hall), the Wesleyan Methodists (a stable loft) and the Bible Christians. Say the authors of a worthy little book, *The West Somerset Mineral Railway* (1962), 'the three congregations seem to have attended each other's outings with a refreshing lack of religious bigotry. . . . Each June the Bible Christians celebrated the anniversary of their chapel's foundation with special services and a tea, and an extra train often had to be provided to convey friends from as far away at Watchet, while the mission church and the Wesleyans held similar Sunday School anniversaries . . .

'Brendon Hill had no doctor (the nearest was at Roadwater) but boasted a midwife. The mining company employed two surgeons to look after the men (one at Watchet and one on the Hill), but the lack of any income when the breadwinner could not work was a constant worry. To encourage thrift for such eventualities a Penny Bank had been opened as early as September 1860, and in 1871 an Accident Fund was started which paid 12s a week to disabled members.'

The village also had a Temperance Society, a Teetotal Fife and Drum Band, a choir and a Band of Hope. The Fife and Drum Band accompanied the first passenger train from Watchet to Combe Row on 4 September 1865. Cheering crowds gathered in every little station en route, and all the shops in Watchet were closed for the holiday. Almost everyone who could travel converged on Combe Row for tea. Combe Row, at the foot of the hills, was the terminus for passenger traffic. Passengers were allowed to go up the incline to the village on the hill, and a truck was fitted with plank seats to cater for them, but they went entirely at their own risk. Those who lived on the hill were entitled to free passes. At the height of the mining activity the railway carried more than 19,000 passengers a year.

During the 1870s thirteen or fourteen mines were in production, and from 1874 to 1878 the output averaged 40,000 tons of ore annually. By the middle of that decade, however, a recession, coinciding with the availability of cheap imported ore, was beginning to herald the doom of the Brendon mines. Mine after mine closed, the Ebbw Vale Company almost ceased steel production, and on 10 May 1879, the mines were officially shut down. Only a week's notice was given, and many of the miners, with nowhere to go and no alternative employment available, suffered considerable distress.

Later in that year there was a revival of trade, and the mines, reopened, staggered on for another four years. Then, in 1883, the venture came to an end, and the machinery and equipment were dismantled and sold off. The railway continued to run a passenger service till 1899, and then that too was closed.

A second revival occurred in 1907. Several of the mines were reopened and the railway started in service again. The venture was short-lived, coming to an end in the following year. Again the railway managed to provide a service of sorts after the mines had closed, but the enterprise was financially hopeless, and its entire assets, including the track itself, were sold by auction in August 1924.

The story is so recent that, naturally, many traces of it may still be seen. Ruins are scattered over the bleak hilltop, and cuttings, sidings and embankments are still features of the landscape. Iron and other minerals are still to be found in the Brendons, and it is therefore not impossible that industry and people may again return to the hills.

Exmoor, divided from the Brendons by the narrow valley of the Quarme, has a parallel history of mineral exploitation in the nineteenth and twentieth centuries. In the 1850s the same ironmasters of South Wales became interested in iron deposits near Simonsbath. Mining began, and a hill railway, on the same pattern as the Brendon Hill one, from Simonsbath to Porlock, was planned and started. Little came of it at the time. The iron mines were closed by 1860, were reopened briefly in the first decade of the present century and closed finally in 1914.

There are still lodes of iron ore, and also of copper and other minerals, in the Exmoor hills. They may yet be worked again, as they have at intervals throughout the centuries. The Dumnonii exploited them before the legions came to Britain; the Romans may have done so, though there is no definite proof; and iron was extracted again by a mining venture in the seventeenth century.

Mining has been the only industry other than agriculture to take any root on Exmoor, and agriculture has to be of a specialized sort, depending largely on grass, for the greater part of the area is above the 1,000-foot contour line. Although many maps designate the region as 'Exmoor Forest', the term 'forest' is used in its old sense, as a chase subject to forest laws, and not to denote a wooded area. Indeed, early in the nineteenth century a Royal Commission could find only 37 trees on the whole of Exmoor, and those were in the valley at Simonsbath. Now many of the combes, especially in the vicinity of the villages, are well wooded, and there are also shelter-belts of trees on the summits. In the Exmoor National Park, which includes the Brendons as well as Exmoor proper, the Forestry Commission alone has 3,000 acres, though not all wooded, of course; and there are several private estates growing timber commercially.

Though much of Exmoor's moorland remains, and at midsummer is aglow with heavy-scented heather, much of it is now enclosed grazing land, with boundary walls of stone often surmounted by beech trees. For this development the Knight family, who were active in the first half of the nineteenth century, can claim chief credit and responsibility. From headquarters at Simonsbath John Knight, who acquired most of his estate in 1818 and eventually owned more than 15,000 acres, created new farms and fields, built new farmhouses, and laid down nearly 30 miles of new roads. Before his time, there were virtually no roads, and pack-horses were the chief form of transport.

As a demonstration of what can be done on these western hills by modern farming, the Ministry of Agriculture has an Experimental Husbandry Farm at Liscombe, at an altitude of about 1,000 feet and with an average rainfall of about 60 inches annually. The farm keeps 440 cattle and 920 sheep on 495 acres, relying chiefly on silage for winter feed. This, of course, is much better than could be achieved in mediaeval times, but even then the unimproved moorland carried a remarkably heavy stock of sheep. Geoffrey Sinclair, in his monograph *The Vegetation of Exmoor*, records a stock of 40,000 sheep on the moors in 1592, which represents two sheep per acre, and he states that this is probably less than the peak in the great days of the wool trade in the fourteenth century. He suggests that this heavy stocking rate may well have resulted in the destruction of the heather and its replacement by Molinia grass, which is still dominant over about 10,000 acres.

Just how this rather intensive use of the moor as a sheep walk was reconciled with its function as a royal hunting forest is obscure, but Exmoor did remain as a possession of the crown until the time of the Commonwealth. It was then sold to a London merchant, James Boevy, who ran into serious trouble with his neighbours around Simonsbath for trying to reclaim the moor and so interfere with their traditional rights. During the centuries the local farmers had acquired certain rights, such as that of pasturing so many ponies on the moor, and were, as elsewhere in England, decidedly reluctant to relinquish them.

In the end, enclosure legislation worked here much as elsewhere. The Crown reserved about 22,000 acres, when the day of division finally came, and most of the commoners got miserable little holdings of from 12 to 31 acres around the margins of the moors. The man who came off next-best to the Crown was Sir Thomas Acland, who already owned extensive estates in the vicinity and who was granted over 3,000 acres. Largely by reason of his local position he had been Warden of the Forest, and the award was on the principle of compensation for loss of income, or, as we might now term it, redundancy pay.

The Aclands were a great hunting family and did much to establish the tradition of stag-hunting on Exmoor. Some authorities maintain that this tradition has much to do with the survival on Exmoor of the largest herd of red deer in England. The case is put by E. R. Lloyd, in his monograph on *The Wild Deer of Exmoor*:

'In the year 1825, after a period of some seventy years of fairly efficient hunting, the pack of hounds then in existence was sold out of the country to Germany, and for the next thirty years there was either none or very little organized hunting of the deer. The result was that by 1855, when a successful attempt was made to restart a pack of hounds in the district, the herd had been reduced to about 50 animals in the whole of the West Country; and according to reliable witnesses of the time, most of all of these remaining deer carried evidence of wounding by rifle or shotgun at some time or another. There can be no doubt at all that if hunting had not been reinstated to something like its former prosperity—which soon became greatly enhanced—the wild red deer on Exmoor and in the surrounding districts would have disappeared for ever well before 1900. As it was, the Devon and Somerset Staghounds were formed on a sound working basis, and by 1900 there were three packs of hounds in the district, hunting a total of eight days a week, and even then the numbers of deer were creeping up all the time.'

The explanation is, of course, that deer do a lot of damage on farms at the edge of the moorland, and, in the absence of any organized hunt (in which the farmers themselves participate), the farmers tend to shoot them.

Nevertheless, the activities of the hounds often get bad publicity in the Press, and there is strong anti-hunting sentiment (though not very noticeable on Exmoor!). Monica Hutchings, in her book *Inside Somerset*, gives the conservationists' point of view when drawing attention to a reserve for hunted deer:

'Just outside Dulverton is the deer sanctuary of Baronsdown, where land owned and maintained by those opposed to the hunting of the wild red deer (both stags and hinds) is kept open as a refuge for hunted, wounded and maimed animals. This is a most humane and up-to-date undertaking on behalf of some of our finest wild animals and merits the support of enlightened nature lovers.'

In 1944 Sir Richard Acland gave 9,848 acres of his family estate to the National Trust, and this has become the nucleus, augmented by purchase and by other gifts, of the 12,400-acre Holnicote Estate which includes some of the loveliest and wildest parts of Exmoor, including more than 6,700 acres of moorland. The Trust also has nearly 1,300 acres on Winsford Hill, south-east of Exford.

Exford is one of the best centres for exploring the western hills and has several small and convenient hotels. It is a delightfully pretty spot, with spectacular moorland all around, though the village itself is shut in by hedges and sunken lanes. Simonsbath, away to the west in one of the remotest parts of Exmoor, is one of the newest villages of Exmoor, for when John Knight came on the scene it was little more than a farmhouse and accessory buildings. The church dates from only 1865. Another oasis in the moors is formed by the little village of Withypool, where once one of Somerset's favourite and best-loved writers on rural matters, Walter Raymond, born in 1852 at Yeovil, lived.

And, of course, on the northern side of the moor there is Oare, much visited by tourists who want to see where Lorna Doone stood when she was shot by the vindictive Carver Doone. Were the Doones real people? Yes, indeed they were, as was Jan Ridd, who went to school at Blundell's, Tiverton. But the story is R. D. Blackmore's, and one must not look for too much historical accuracy in a work which, after all, is both a novel and a masterpiece.

Isolated from the rest of Somerset, and geographically belonging to Devon, the little town of Dulverton, on the Barle, lies south of the moors and just across the county boundary from Bampton, where the Exmoor ponies are sold at the annual fair. Dulverton had a Norman castle—Mounsey, on an adjacent hill—and once a mine for silver and lead. Here was born Sir George Williams, who founded the Y.M.C.A.

Exmoor itself is particularly rich in barrows, stone circles, menhirs and other formations of the Neolithic period, and of the succeeding Bronze Age. Identified tumuli number between three and four hundred. There are stone circles on Withypool Hill and on the hills above Porlock, though they are poor little things, with many of their stones missing, compared to such monuments as Stonehenge. On Wilmersham Common, on East Pinford (near Badgworthy), and on Little Tom's Hill near by are parallel rows of standing stones, like those of Carnac but very much smaller, both in numbers and in size. Most of them protrude only a foot or two from the ground. Solitary standing stones are numerous, one of the largest being Challacombe Longstone, which stands 9 feet 6 inches high, but it is difficult to determine which are of genuine antiquity and which have been erected within the past few centuries, as rubbing posts for cattle, boundary marks or other purposes. The barrows are mostly bowl barrows, belonging to the culture known as the Beaker Folk. One found by chance on Bampfylde Hill, near North Molton, in 1917 contained a necklace of beads in which both amber and Egyptian blue faience work were represented, as have also been discovered in similar barrows on Salisbury Plain. A connection, of some sort, between the West Country and the eastern Mediterranean in the fourteenth century B.C. is thus established.

Exmoor has 20 or 30 hill forts, probably dating from the Iron Age, or the last three of four hundred years B.C., but none has so far been excavated, and some of the most impressive are over the county boundary, in Devonshire. Elworthy Barrows, on the eastern spur of the Brendons, is an unusually large earthwork which, for some unexplained reason, was never finished. There are also hill forts, such as Dowsborough and Ruborough on the Quantocks.

Evidence of Roman occupation of the western hills is scarce. Earlier we have taken note of Vespasian's campain in the West

Country in the years following the Roman invasion of A.D. 43, but resistance probably petered out after the *oppida* of central Somerset had fallen. However, the Silures, across the Bristol Channel in South Wales, were not conquered for another 30 years, and raiding across the sea seems to have been a threat that the Romans took seriously. One of the few Roman remains on Exmoor therefore is the small earthwork known as Old Burrow, on the hills by the Devon–Somerset boundary near County Gate. It was garrisoned, temporarily, by about 80 legionaries under a centurion, until the danger had passed.

Also on the moors are numbers of small enclosures with quite formidable stone ramparts, which are thought to be the sites of fortified farms in the Dark Ages, though again none has been excavated. The best-known relic of that period, however, is the *Caratacus Stone*, which stands on Winsford Hill and bears the inscription '*Carataci nepus*', translated as 'a descendant of Caratacus'. This could be the Caratacus whose defiance of the Romans is recorded in most history books, but Caratacus, or Caradoc, was a common Celtic name. The stone is, however, an authentic relic of the 5th or early 6th century A.D.

The Saxons seem to have occupied Exmoor during or just after the reign of the West Saxon king Ina, whom we have met on several occasions. Most of the village place-names of the western hills are Saxon, though some are Celtic. Some of the Saxon villages, such as one near Badgworthy, were abandoned during the Middle Ages.

Ancient trackways abound on the moors, one of them running the entire length of the main ridge of the Brendons and Exmoor. Many of these tracks cross the numerous streams by means of clapper bridges, which, roughly, are flat stones placed atop upright ones. The best-known multiple clapper bridge is Tarr Steps, visited by thousands of tourists each summer. It carries an ancient road across the river Barle below Winsford Hill and is supposed by most visitors to be prehistoric. Most authorities think, however, that it is more likely to be mediaeval.

9. The Somerset Coast

To old-time mariners approaching England from the Atlantic, the Bristol Channel was the 'wrong channel'. Carry on a few score of miles too far north before you turned right and you landed up on the rocks of the north Cornwall or north Devon coast instead of sailing smoothly along the English Channel. For those familiar with the route, however, it offered easy access to England's back-door (or, as Bristol people would doubtless have it, England's front-door). You were in Bristol by the time you would be off the Isle of Wight, and no French privateers to bother you.

From very early times the western sea-route was known and used. More than one prehistoric culture seems, from archaeological evidence, to have spread over the country from the south-west, the inference being that it came from western France or Spain. And sea traffic across the narrow seas between Wales and Southern Ireland and the south-west peninsula of Britain went on all the time. Even the well-known 'blue stones' which form one of the circles of Stonehenge are thought to have been brought from the Prescelly Mountains of Pembrokeshire by sea and river.

In the last chapter we took note of two episodes illustrating traffic across the sea between west Somerset and South Wales. In the second half of the nineteenth century iron ore was shipped from Watchet to Newport in Monmouthshire for eventual transport to the blast furnaces of Ebbw Vale. And 1,800 years earlier the Romans established garrisons on Exmoor to guard against raids by the Silures of South Wales. We shall come across numerous similar examples as we move along the coast.

The three main divisions of Somerset which we have already defined are well illustrated in the county's coastline. They are the hilly west, the central levels and the varied north with its turmoil of hills and valleys. From the Devon border to the mouth of the Parret the coast runs almost due west to east; then it turns at approximately a right angle and veers away to the north.

A notable characteristic of the Somerset coast is its prodigious tides, which have enabled Bristol, a city seven or eight miles inland on a rather narrow river, to become a great port. The same factors govern the port of Bridgwater, which is about the same distance from the sea as the crow flies but considerably farther if one has to follow the tortuous course of the river. The Parret, like the Severn, has a 'bore', or miniature tidal wave, which rushes up the river, its height depending on wind, tide and season, and makes its presence felt as far up as Langport.

As we have seen in the chapter on the Levels, the coastline of this central sector was in early times an indistinct frontier. The heartland of Somerset was amphibious territory—an island-studded expanse of marshland liable to frequent invasion by the sea. In a wet winter the flood area could extend virtually to the Dorset border (along the Yeo, north of Yeovil), and cut Somerset in half. Some of the inland towns of which we have already taken note were therefore ports in early times—Glastonbury, for instance, and Langport until very recently.

Beginning our coastal survey in the far west, we find the first potential small port, Porlock, cosily inland, which seems to be a reminder of the days when the sea was a highway for dangerous men rather than for commerce. Indeed, Porlock had its share of excitement in the centuries when England was being moulded. Its inhabitants beat off a vigorous attack by Danish pirates in the year 918, and in 1052 it was raided and set on fire by Saxon Harold, who was subsequently king but who was then in exile in Ireland. Apparently, however, here it is the sea which has retreated, leaving an expanse of silty meadow where once the tides rolled.

Porlock is best known to travellers for the tremendous hill which leads out of it up to Exmoor—a hill notorious for its engine-testing gradients. Under its shelter Porlock enjoys an almost Mediterranean climate, seldom depreciated by frost or snow. It is a pleasant little place. The dedication of its ancient church, to St Dubricius, is another reminder of the cross-Channel traffic with Wales, for this saint was a bishop of Llandaff, who died in the year 612. He and a St Culbone came here on a missionary journey. A legend says that he crowned Arthur king of Britain, but that is unlikely, there being no evidence that Arthur ever had that title. The tomb of Sir John Harington in the church (he died in 1418) is reckoned to be one of the finest of such memorials in Somerset.

St Culbone gave his name to the little village of Culbone, about two miles westward along the hilly coast. The mediaeval church is one of the smallest in England, being only 35 feet by 12 feet.

As we have noted in the preceding chapter, plans to make Porlock an important port were formulated in the mid-nineteenth century. A railway to bring down iron ore from Exmoor for shipment to South Wales was begun, but nothing came of it. Now the little town's chief industry is its summer tourist trade.

The towering buttress of North Hill, which rises to 1,014 feet, stands between Porlock and Minehead and forces the road inland. On the way, a slight detour from the main road takes us into the village of Selworthy, surely one of the loveliest villages in England. Its thatched cottages and flower gardens, with the wooded slopes leading up to Exmoor, have featured on many a calendar and picture postcard. The view from the door of the fifteenth-century church, with Dunkery Beacon as its focal point in the distance, is superb. Near by is a fifteenth-century tithe barn and a damaged stone cross of about a century later.

Allerford, an even smaller village off the same road, is likewise well blessed with picturesque cottages and has a fine two-arched stone bridge for packhorses.

Both Selworthy and Allerford are noted for their walnut trees, but the king of all was the giant walnut (felled in 1953) of Bossington, the third of these villages behind Porlock Bay. It too has thatched cottages and a tiny tumbling stream. North Hill, by the way, is sometimes known as Bossington Beacon and sometimes as Selworthy Beacon—it is all the same hill.

Minehead is one of the oldest towns in Somerset. Its name was anciently spelt 'Mynett' and is probably of Celtic derivation, from *'mynedd'*, meaning 'a hill'. And on its hill stands St Michael's church, as it has for 500 years, a beacon light in its tower serving as a guide for ships approaching harbour. St Michael is, of course, a saint associated with high hills and towers, and we have already noticed dedications to him on Glastonbury Tor and on the hill at Montacute.

Early references to Minehead feature the expected cross-Channel traffic. One recorded episode tells how in 1265 a force of Welshmen descended on the town and did an immense amount of damage before being roundly defeated by troops from Dunster. A deputation which asked the Queen Elizabeth I for help in constructing a new pier stated that the old pier had become so shaky that soon 'no shippe nor bote can take succour there. The decay of an ancient and daily passage from the partys of Glamorgan in Wales to your said Piere, by mene of which the faires and markets of your countie have ever been furnished with no small number of cattle, shepe, woole, varne, clothe, butter, stone, coal, oysteres, salmon and other sundrie kinds of fish and flesh to the losses of your majestys customs there. . . .'

The list of commodities is interesting, and the fact that there was a daily service even more so. Much of the trade in wool was with Ireland, and, in later centuries, with the Mediterranean. The town's arms show a sailing ship and a woolpack. At one time, too, Minehead had a considerable commerce in herrings, exporting up to 4,000 barrels a year, but the herrings forsook the Bristol Channel and Irish Sea waters suddenly, and the trade ceased.

The Luttrell family of Dunster had Minehead very much under their wing for centuries. It was a Sir Hugh Luttrell in the fifteenth century who built a fine new pier there, and George Luttrell who did much the same in 1616, his pier being incorporated in the present harbour structure. In the seventeenth century the port developed a ship-building trade, and in 1701 Minehead shipowners had no fewer than 30 ships at sea. Decline came towards the end of the century, and when, in 1830, the Reform Bill was passed, Minehead, which had been sending two members to Parliament, was disenfranchised as a rotten borough.

In the era of pleasure steamers, from the 1890s to the Second World War, boatloads of visitors arrived almost daily during the summer from such ports as Bristol and Newport, but the new promenade pier built in 1901 for their benefit had to be dismantled during the war. Nowadays privately owned yachts, dinghies and fishing boats are the vessels most frequently seen in the harbour.

Minehead, however, continues to enjoy a measure of prosperity as a holiday resort. In recent years it has acquired a Butlin's Holiday Camp, a prospect which was viewed with misgivings by many of the inhabitants but which has fitted into the environment with very little fuss, besides bringing welcome trade.

Dunster, a few miles eastward on the Bridgwater road and a mile inland, has so much to offer in the way of beauty, character and quaintness that it is often submerged in summer by weight of tourists. Dominating it is a mediaeval castle which, in appearance, is everything that one imagines a mediaeval castle should be. It belongs to the Luttrell family, who purchased the estate in 1376 and are still in residence, making the castle one of the oldest continuously inhabited houses in England. Before that William de Mohun, who was granted the estate at the Conquest, built a Norman castle here, but of that edifice nothing remains.

The town also possesses a splendid church, dating mostly from the fifteenth century, which once served a Benedictine priory there— at least in part, for the church was divided into two, one part for the monks and one for Dunster's citizens. The church has a lofty tower, like so many others in Somerset, and some magnificent marble memorials to members of the Luttrell family. The church bells chime hymn tunes.

In Dunster's broad main street is its covered Yarn Market, built by George Luttrell about 1600. Here the smooth kersey cloth, manufactured at Dunster, was once displayed for sale. Near by the mediaeval Luttrell Arms inn was probably once a town residence of the Abbot of Cleeve. A row of cottages of unusual architecture, with overhanging slates beneath the windows of each storey, is known as 'The Nunnery', but mistakenly, for Dunster never had a nunnery, though the building may have been used as a guest house for the priory.

Dunster was the scene of much action during the Civil War. The Luttrells were for Parliament and for a year held their castle against Royalist attacks. In 1643 they had to surrender, and Royalist troops then remained in occupation until 1646. Prince Charles, afterwards Charles II, visited it during these years, and the room he slept in still bears his name. By 1645 Dunster Castle was the only Royalist stronghold left in Somerset. It was attacked with great determination by Blake at the end of the year, but the garrison, under Colonel Francis Windham, fought back resolutely, and it was not until April 1646, that it finally surrendered. Traces of the battle, such as a hole made by a cannon-shot in a rafter of the Yarn Market, may still be seen.

A well-known picture of Dunster Castle was painted by Turner. It is from a little hill near Carhampton, the next village along the coast. In Carhampton itself, the interior of the church is well worth a visit, for it contains a magnificent rood screen, still splendidly painted in vivid colours. Carhampton, too, is one of the only two places in Somerset where the ancient custom of Wassailing the Apple Trees every January is still kept.

Washford, at the approaches to Watchet, lies in a valley called in old times *Vallis Florida*, 'the Flowery Valley'. Here, with their unerring eye for the beautiful and fertile, the Cistercians in the twelfth century built an abbey, Cleeve Abbey. Little is known of its history, and it was not a large establishment, for only 17 monks were in residence at the time of the Dissolution. Perhaps because it was a quiet and peaceable place it was not unduly ransacked when it passed out of monastic hands, and many of the buildings remain little damaged. The church has gone, but the refectory, dormitory, dining room and many other features are intact.

Between Cleeve Abbey and the coast Chapel Cleeve has a grange, now a house, which is probably on the site of the ancient Chapel of Our Lady of Cleeve, much visited by mediaeval pilgrims.

Watchet we have already visited as the terminus of the West Somerset Mineral Railway, which brought down iron ore from Brendon Hill. A new pier was built for the traffic, enabling the ore to be tipped straight into the holds of ships anchored by the jetty. About the same time another railway line, the Bristol and Exeter, also extended its services to Watchet, which henceforth for half a century or so enjoyed a period of happy prosperity. Unfortunately, the decline of the iron-ore trade coincided with two tremendous gales, one in late December 1900, and the other in September 1903, which smashed the harbour and destroyed a number of ships anchored there. The harbour has since been rebuilt and improved, and a new trade is developing. Supplies for a paper mill at Watchet are largely brought in by sea.

In an earlier age Watchet was an important Saxon port, which was attacked and burnt by the Danes on at least three occasions. In the sixteenth century a Royal Commission noted that Watchet was a port trading in salt and wine, presumably from France, and in the next century it was recorded as having a trade with Ireland. It also developed, in the seventeenth century, a trade with Bristol in burnt kelp, used in the manufacture of glass.

Watchet's fifteenth-century church is dedicated to St Decuman, another of those Welsh saints who in the Dark Ages came drifting over from Wales on a raft, together with a cow to supply him with milk.

This is the family seat of the Windhams, who have played a prominent part in west Somerset history and whose memorials enrich the church. It was also the home (the exact place was Orchard, a hamlet near by), of Robert Fitzurse, one of the murderers of Thomas a'Becket. And it is supposed to have been the home port of Coleridge's *Ancient Mariner*.

A mile or so along the coast, westwards, Blue Anchor is developing into a seaside resort, with a useful expanse of sands and, inevitably, a caravan park.

East Quantoxhead, to the east of Watchet, is a haven of rural peace, just off the busy A39 high road. The little clusters of thatched cottages leading to and grouped around a tree-hung pond with ducks (there is always one white one) paddling on it make a scene so exactly corresponding to the picture of Old England which we create in our minds that it seems too good to be true, and, for an unworthy moment, we wonder whether Walt Disney has not had a hand in it. This is still Luttrell territory, the fifteenth-century Court being occupied by members of the family, as it has been ever since it was built. They are the direct descendants of one Paganel, who held it at the time of the Norman Conquest. The estate must be one of the few bits of England that have never changed hands, by purchase, and have remained with the same family for nearly 1,000 years. The church is delightfully situated by the garden wall of the manor house and is approached by a rising path through lawns and flower-beds.

Nearby West Quantoxhead is locally known as St Audries, after the church dedication to St Audrey (or St Etheldreda, to give her her full name). A little stream which twinkles through the meadows and under the great trees finds its way into the sea by tumbling over the edge of a cliff. Under the sea here is a submerged forest, the trunks of whose trees may still be seen. The tusks of a mammoth excavated from the beach are now in Taunton Museum.

And so, through a group of tiny, undistinguished but quietly attractive villages, including Kilve, Lilstock, Otterhampton and Stolford, we follow a coast that lies ever flatter to the mouth of the Parret. Here, on a coast which long remained as desolate and un-visited as any corner of England, claimed only by sea-birds, fisher-men and cattle, the great nuclear power station of Hinkley Point appears to grow up abruptly from the sea-bed. A better site could hardly have been found, for, apart from the consideration that the Parret estuary provides an unlimited supply of water for cooling, the massive squareness of the towering rectangular buildings seems somehow to match the austere horizontal lines of an otherwise featureless landscape.

The effect of the Bristol Channel's huge tides here on this flat coast is to create a vast amphibious no-man's-land of silt and sand. Over the Stert Flats the sea at low tide recedes for three or four miles and then comes galloping back at an alarming pace. The Parret cuts a winding, deep-water channel between the Flats and the similar Gore Sands which swerve northwards towards Brean Down.

Rev. William Greswell, historian of the Quantocks in the early years of this century, describes the scene:

'At low water the estuary is wide and glittering, reflecting the light in a marvellous fashion when the sunlight plays in flickering fashion upon the smooth ridges, which, like an opaque cloud, seem to give back as much light as they receive. An amphibious region where, nevertheless, man at certain times can neither creep, crawl, walk or swim, and the catastrophe of death follows the fisherman or shrimper who ventures carelessly on it in the half-lights of a win-ter's afternoon.'

The men of the coastal villages have, however, devised a kind of vehicle which enables them to traverse the flats when fishing or shrimping. It is known as a 'mud-horse' and is a sort of sledge on wooden runners which spreads their weight and so enables them to skim over the surface, propelled by their feet.

A mile or so out from Stert Point, opposite Burnham, lies the ephemeral Stert Island. It came into existence through a shifting of tide and current probably in the eighteenth century and in recent years has been eroded at a rapid rate. Elsewhere along this unstable shore, however, the land is winning in the eternal war. In 1928 some experimental consignments of Spartina grass were brought from Poole Harbour, to see how effectively plantings of it could trap the silt and prevent the incessant scouring by the tides. The experiment proved so successful that more plantings were made, and the grass now extends for more than two miles along the shore and a quarter of a mile or so seawards. As the grass takes root and stabilizes the soil so other plants are enabled to establish themselves, and in places the level of the foreshore has been raised by more than six feet.

More than 6,000 acres of the foreshore and flats are now the Bridgwater Bay Nature Reserve, established in 1954 and frequented by hordes of waterfowl.

A few miles inland the first village on the western bank of the Parret, Combwich, has provided a favourite topic for controversy by antiquarians. Here in times past was the last ford over the river, which at this point has as its bed 'a smooth layer of blue lias stones, across which at low water it has been possible for horsemen or wheeled traffic to pass'. There was also a ferry, extensively used for both passenger traffic and the transport of goods and cattle. It also served at times as an outlying port of Bridgwater, for boats large enough to mistrust the hazards of river navigation any farther.

As we have noted on page 116, Combwich is the likeliest site for the victory of the Saxons of 'Kynuit'. At various times in the past 100 or so years large numbers of ancient skeletons have been unearthed below the old fort at Combwich, indicating that a considerable battle was fought there at some time or another.

We now cross the estuary and begin our journey northwards. Here we are back on the central levels, the sea coast of Sedgemoor and the peat moors towards Glastonbury. They are crossed nowadays by wide, deep channels from which pumping stations discharge surplus water into others even wider and deeper, to carry it off to the sea. The latest acquisition of this sort is the Huntspill river, cut in 1940 primarily to supply water to a new explosives factory at Puriton.

The grazing on these levels is extraordinarily rich, especially in the neighbourhood of Pawlett, known as the Pawlett Hams. From the cattle fattened on these superb pastures aristocratic graziers of the late Middle Ages and Stuart times grew rich. A slight ridge at Pawlett marks the opposite side of the old ford at Combwich Passage, once a crossing on the main highway from Bristol to the West. Now a new western highway, the M5, is driving its way across the levels, with, it seems, a maximum disturbance by heavy machinery, though doubtless in time it will be satisfactorily absorbed into the complaisant Somerset landscape.

The northern boundary of the Huntspill Levels (though almost exactly similar country extends on the other side and is known as the Burnham Levels) may be taken as the river Brue. This is the river which we first met at Bruton and which flows past Glastonbury, near which town it used to lose itself in a vast morass. Its waters, hastened on their way by many artificial cuts and drains, find their way to the sea just beyond Highbridge, a town as unromantic in appearance as its name suggests. The high bridge originally served the dual purpose of bridge and dam, for it had sluice gates which were shut when the tide came in. Quite large boats could therefore come in with their cargo and berth almost alongside the road. From Highbridge in the 1830s a canal was dug to Glastonbury, giving the old town a new water link with the sea. It lasted for only 20 years, however, and was closed when the railways took over. More recently Highbridge has become a notorious bottleneck on the A38 high road, and the opening of the M5 will be a relief to motorists and Highbridge citizens alike.

West of the main road Highbridge merges with Burnham-on-Sea, most of which is a featureless region of Victorian red-brick terraced houses. Its sea-front is elegant, genteel and somewhat dreary. Twice a day, at low tide, the sea tiptoes away almost out of sight over the western horizon.

Until late in the eighteenth century Burnham was a thinly populated, poverty-stricken village of farmers and graziers. Then a curate of the church, Rev. David Davies, had the idea that the rocks beneath it ought to hold mineral springs, as at Cheltenham, Harrogate and elsewhere. He accordingly started sinking wells, obtaining much of the money from a lighthouse which he built on the treacherous shoals at the mouth of the Brue, and for the services of which he was able, by means which are not at all clear, to exact a toll from passing ships. A few springs, of doubtful value, were found, and small groups of houses were built as a nucleus of the potential spa. They never amounted to much, except that they attracted attention to Burnham as a seaside resort, as which it developed throughout Victoria's reign. At one time it had a passenger ship service, by paddle-steamer, connecting it with Bridgwater and South Wales. While there is nothing exciting about Burnham, it has certain quiet attractions, as Monica Hutchings says, making the best of it; 'Mendip and Quantock are in sight, the air is bracing, and the sunsets across Steep and Flat Holm would satisfy a Turner'.

The road northwards from Burnham to Brean Down is one that I often travel. Through Berrow and Brean it goes, reasonably straight, for there is little scope for meandering, with a ridge of sand-dunes hiding the sea on the left and a growing series of caravan sites behind banks and hedges on the right. From this flat shore the towering rampart of Brean Down looms like a mountain and thrusts a mile or so out into the Channel like the Rock of Gibraltar.

Brean Down, an outcrop of the Mendips, provides an exhilarating clifftop walk of a mile or so, at an altitude of about 200 feet. The springy turf on the summit is still close-cropped by rabbits, despite myxomatosis, and in May carpets of bluebells bloom among the unfolding bracken. National Trust property and a nature reserve, it used to harbour a nesting pair of peregrine falcons and still has two or three pairs of ravens, as well as innumerable sea-birds. It is also almost the only British site of the white rock-rose, though here it is far from rare.

Splendid views may be enjoyed from the top of the hill. Southwards the broad sands stretch away to a horizon around the mouth of the Parret, and at the foot of the cliffs they are so firm that cars are allowed to park on them, for picnickers and for bathers who are hardy enough to chase the tide for a mile or two or patient enough to wait for it to come in. Sand-yachting is a sport enjoyed here from time to time. On the northern side the tidal flats, equally extensive, look blacker and more slippery. Anglers based on Weston who fish from the rocks beneath the Down delay departure for as long as possible and then tempt Neptune by trekking, by well-marked but apparently interminable paths, to safety across the tide-threatened sands.

Weston, looking from this vantage-point like a Mediterranean seaside resort, seems little more than a stone's throw away (it is, to be precise, about a couple of miles across the bay), but before we go down there are a few places to be visited on the levels behind the coast road. By coming directly to Brean Down along the shore we have by-passed East Brent and Brent Knoll, which last is an abrupt hill rising like another Brean Down above the marshes.

Brent Knoll is, as a matter of fact, considerably higher than Brean, rising to an altitude of 450 feet. It is a conspicuous landmark from

South Wales, on the other side of the Bristol Channel and is probably better known by sight, if not by name, than the similar tor of Glastonbury. In early ages it must have been an island and therefore, by every standard, an ideal site for a hill fort. Its fortifications, dating from the Iron Age, enclose about four acres. This may well have been one of the western hill towns subdued by Vespasian, and it is thought to have been re-occupied in the Dark Ages and to have been used again by the West Saxons during the Danish wars. Under the south-eastern scarp of the hill the name of the hamlet of Battle-borough is suggestive.

Brent Knoll village, also known as South Brent, on the south-western slopes of the hill, has in its church, appropriately dedicated like so many hill churches to St Michael, an amusing satire on a mediaeval ecclesiastical squabble, perpetuated in bench-ends. The quarrel was evidently between the parish priest and the Abbot of Glastonbury, and, rather surprisingly, the priest won. So a local wood-carver commemorated the victory. The Abbot is depicted as a fox, dressed in ecclesiastical robes, with crook and mitre, to ensure that there is no mistake about his identity. He is lording it over a collection of birds and animals, including several geese. Next we see the revolt, with the fox being put into the stocks, having first been stripped of his robes and his mitre. Lastly he is hanged, with the geese hauling at the rope. It is a series of cartoons of which any artist might be proud.

From Brent we can gaze back south-eastwards over the levels to the village of Mark, its elegant, tall tower a landmark for many miles. It played an important part in the affairs of the mediaeval Abbots of Glastonbury, being a key point in the network of waterways which linked the basins of the Brue and the Axe, most of which were devised and constructed by the abbots for their own benefit.

Continuing northwards, we encounter another outcrop of the Mendips in Bleadon Hill, which must have been almost an island in prehistoric times. It lies directly across the levels from Brean Down, with the smaller and lower hill of Uphill in between. Its triangular massif, about three miles by two, is ringed with villages, while tumuli and the outlines of Celtic fields pattern its slopes and undisturbed sections of its summit.

Bleadon has no major earthwork of its own, but Banwell, on the isthmus of hills which links Bleadon with the main range of the Mendips, has an unusual one. Within the small banked enclosure near the hilltop fort known as Banwell Camp is a turf cross, about ten feet wide, raised two feet above ground level, and with arms of 72 feet and 56 feet. No one has yet been able to give a satisfactory explanation of it.

Banwell Camp itself was doubtless a satellite fort of the great earthwork of Dolebury, four miles to the east along the northern escarpment of Mendip. This hill fortress, covering 20 acres, was somewhat unusual in having massive stone walls.

Banwell has one of those splendid Somerset churches with a lofty tower, this one rising to over 100 feet. Its interior is equally magnificent, with painted roof, a finely carved Tudor doorway, a superb chancel screen and much lovely stonework. The building now known as The Abbey is the fifteenth-century manor house of the Bishop of Wells.

Churchill, a large village under Dolebury Camp, was the original home of the Churchills, ancestors of the Dukes of Marlborough and of Sir Winston. There are many memorials to the family in the fifteenth-century church. Though the setting of Churchill is still satisfactorily rural, we are now within a dozen miles of Bristol and so inside the commuter belt. We have digressed to visit it and must now return westwards to see Weston-super-Mare.

Weston is entirely modern. A century or two ago it was an obscure village of only about 100 inhabitants. Now it is one of the busiest and most popular seaside resorts of the West Country, largely because it is so easily accessible from the Midlands. It also possesses the normal asset of this coast, a vast expanse of sand, safe for children, and a shallow sea for them to bathe in, though it has had to instal swimming pools to cater for bathers when the tide is out. Little is lacking, too, in the range of the usual seaside amusements, such as pleasure arcades, theatres, cinemas, shops, bingo halls, donkeys on the sands and pleasure boats. There are parks and gardens, and fine views across the Severn to Flatholm and Steepholm and of passing ships on their way to and from Avonmouth.

As a seaside resort Weston first began to be developed by Bristol investors, early in the nineteenth century. Its expansion really accelerated, however, with the extension of the Bristol and Exeter railway to the town. Bristol citizens could now come here on day trips to the seaside, and it still remains popular with them.

The town is flanked at its southern end by the rocky hill of Up-hill, at its northern by Worlebury Hill which is a less spectacular edition of Brean Down. Uphill is probably older than Weston, mark-ing as it does the site of a former ferry across the mouth of the river Axe. It is also thought to have been a port for the Roman lead-mines of the Mendips, perhaps the one known as *Axium*. The ruined church of St Nicholas on the hill over the Axe levels is a well-known landmark, much of it dating from Norman times. Within the hill a cave, discovered in 1824, contained the bones of many prehistoric animals, including the elephant, bear, hyena and rhinoceros.

Worlebury on the northern hill spur is an impressive Iron Age earthwork, with traces of hut circles where its former inhabitants lived. The hill is sheltered on its northern slopes by pleasant woods, through which a picturesque path leads down to the village of Kewstoke. Off the tip of the headland the rocky islet of Birnbeck used to be the centre of a flourishing sprat fishery.

Out in the middle of the Channel, marking approximately where the mouth of the Severn becomes the Bristol Channel, are two larger, though still quite small, islands—Flatholm and Steepholm. Both are limestone outcrops of the Mendips, the main range of which is here submerged. Flatholm, the northernmost of the two, is, as its name implies, a flattish island with easy landing. Conse-quently it is frequently visited by excursionists in summer. Offici-ally, however, it belongs to Glamorgan, not to Somerset.

Steepholm, on the Somerset side of the deepwater channel, is much more difficult of access. Indeed, landing is possible only in calm weather. As a nature reserve it is the only British location for the very rare single peony and is also a sanctuary for sea-birds. Recently it has been designated as a memorial reserve to an old colleague of mine, the late Kenneth Allsop, a distinguished natural-ist known to millions through his television appearances.

Both islands have been frequently fortified in time of war, and many of the later fortifications remain. The mother of King Harold took refuge here after her son had been killed at the battle of Hastings. So did the Danes on more than one occasion after defeat by the Saxons. Earlier, Gildas, the Celtic saint and chronicler who was a contemporary of Arthur, used to spend Lent on Steepholm, living, it is said, on gulls' eggs and fish, while his colleague, St

Cadoc, did the same on Flatholm.

Above the islands the channel, or river mouth, is only about ten miles wide and narrowing all the time. Two other seaside resorts, however, are situated on the somewhat muddy shore before the confluence of the Bristol Avon with the Severn. They are Clevedon and Portishead. Both are modern towns grown up around ancient villages.

Clevedon has a fine mediaeval church and a manor house, Clevedon Court, which is one of the most splendid in Somerset, being in the same class as Lyte's Cary and Montacute. It was begun in the reign of Edward II, with considerable additions in Tudor times. Hills shelter the town from the north-east, giving the place a mild climate. It is a pleasant and not unduly commercialized resort, patronized on a day basis by Bristol and other local folk rather than by holiday-makers from farther afield booking for a week or two. Many retired couples have settled here.

Portishead, even farther up the Severn, has given up the search for clean bathing water in the Severn and has installed a spacious heated swimming pool. As elsewhere along this coast, the scenery is good, with hills all around and fine views across the Severn to Monmouthshire. The main current of the river here sweeps close to the Somerset shore, and retired folk sitting in the gardens may enjoy the sight of ships of all sizes passing almost within hailing distance. But Portishead, besides being virtually a seaside suburb of Bristol, has docks of its own, a huge power station and some naval establishments. In the old village, almost submerged by new development, are a number of pleasant old houses around the church which has a typical Somerset tower, and red-brick Portishead Court, the manor house near by, has Elizabethan features. The Wansdyke, that enigmatic earthwork of the Dark Ages, which we have previously encountered near Bath, here reaches the sea, near a point which was fortified in Roman times.

The flat country behind Portishead and Clevedon is known as Gordano, a name thought to be derived from two Celtic words meaning 'marshy valley', which certainly suit it. Four villages on these levels, namely, Clapton, Easton, Weston and Walton, have the suffix 'in-Gordano' attached to them.

The range of hills bordering the valley on the south has on its ridge another Cadbury Camp, an Iron Age earthwork almost as impressive as its namesake in south-east Somerset. Near here in 1922 a hoard of over 3,000 Roman coins was found in a field, and much British pottery has also been unearthed.

Clapton-in-Gordano has a thirteenth-century church, dedicated to St Michael and therefore naturally on a hill. Its Court House is only a little older and displays some unusual features of mediaeval architecture. The thirteenth-century wooden screen, one of the oldest in existence, now in Clapton church once served in Clapton Court.

Weston-in-Gordano has an early mediaeval church, damaged a few years ago by fire, with the unusual feature of a gallery in the porch. This, it is thought, was used by choirboys on special occasions, as for singing the triumphal 'All glory, laud and honour' on Palm Sunday.

Portbury, near the northern entrance to the Gordano valley, was probably a port in Roman times, when the sea claimed more territory there than it now does. It is guarded by another hilltop camp, Celtic in origin but occupied by the Romans, to judge from the numerous remains found from time to time. It once had a priory, annexed to the Augustinian abbey at Bristol.

The Augustinians also had a more important priory farther down the coast, about four miles north of Weston-super-Mare. This is Woodspring Priory, originally Worspring, built in 1210. Its buildings now serve as a farmhouse and farmstead and are still mostly in good condition.

Between the coastal zone of northern Somerset and the hilly fringes of the Mendips lie a group of villages on the approach to Bristol. Busy and thriving nowadays because of their proximity to the great port, they have become almost suburban and are populated very largely by commuters.

Congresbury (pronounced 'Coomsbury') sits on the bank of another river Yeo, which discharges into the Severn between Weston-super-Mare and Clevedon. Yeo is a word which, like Avon, means 'water'; hence its frequent repetition. The village has a fifteenth-century church, with, unusually for Somerset, a spire; an ancient village cross; and several attractive old houses. Its parish hall, with arched stone window-frames, was once the mediaeval vicarage. Above the village, on a hill by the road to Yatton, is yet another Cadbury Camp (the 'Cad' in Cadbury is probably the Celtic word for 'battle'). Its story seems to be parallel to that of Cadbury Castle near South Cadbury, for the hill fort was of Iron Age origin and was apparently occupied again and refortified during the Dark Ages.

Legend has been busy with Congresbury. Its name is said to be derived from St Congar, and the stump of an old yew in the church-yard is still referred to as St Congar's walking-stick. The tale is that Congar was the son of a Byzantine emperor, who wanted to avoid an unwelcome marriage and become a hermit. So he fled to the west and, like Joseph of Arimathea, settled down at a place where his staff budded when stuck in the ground. Also like Joseph he built there a wattle church, which King Ina of Wessex later endowed and provided with enough cash for it to be replaced by a stone one. The date given for these events is around A.D. 711. Another tradi-tion is that Congresbury was the see of an early Christian bishop in Roman times. I am told, too, though I have not seen it, that there is a flowering thorn on Cadbury Hill that blooms at Christmastime, like the one at Glastonbury.

On the other side of the hill Yatton has a Roman villa site on which a fine tesselated pavement was uncovered. Its church is a noble fourteenth-century building with a truncated spire. Among its treasures, in a glass case, is one of the oldest examples of embroidery in England—a funeral pall of blue velvet with figures of saints and Biblical characters.

On the other side of Congresbury, Wrington, already mentioned on page 81, has one of the most magnificent church towers in a county which offers plenty of competition. It rises to 112 feet. The interior of the church is equally impressive, with particularly fine aisle roofs and internal arches. At Wrington, in a cottage known as Barley Wood, lived Hannah More, the philanthropist whose good deeds we have noted at Cheddar and elsewhere. The village was also the birthplace of John Locke, the seventeenth-century philosopher.

The main road from Weston-super-Mare to Bristol (the A370), which passes through part of Congresbury, runs north-eastwards from that village under the scarp of a well-wooded range of hills which goes by several names (Cleeve Hill is one). The pleasant scenery, enjoyed by crowds of Bristolians at week-ends, is enhanced by several deep, dry coombes slashed through the hills, like minia-ture Cheddar Gorges. The largest are Goblin Coombe, near the vil-lage of Cleeve, and Brockley Coombe.

To the left, on the edge of another zone of dead-flat levels so characteristic of Somerset, several large scattered villages spread themselves over the meadows. Nailsea, the most extensive of them, had an industrial development of its own a couple of centuries ago. Coal was discovered and worked. Attracted by the presence of easily acquired fuel, a Bristol glassmaker, John Lucas, moved his glassworks here in the 1780s, and for 100 years Nailsea had a glass factory, making chiefly bottles and window glass. Both glassworks and colliery have long since vanished, and the main employer of labour in the parish is now a cider factory. Nailsea nowadays, however, is mainly a residential suburb of Bristol.

Behind Nailsea and Wraxall the ridge of Failand Hill imposes a barrier between the valley of the Kenn and that of the Avon. It is crowned by Tyntesfield Park, an enormous Victorian Gothic mansion. The main road finds a gap between this ridge and Backwell Hill and sweeps on, past Flax Bourton and Long Ashton into Bristol.

Long Ashton may be reckoned a Somerset suburb of Bristol. Ashton Park, on the opposite side of the Avon Gorge to Clifton, belongs to Bristol Corporation and serves as a green lung for its citizens. The city has not yet, however, found the ideal use for the immense Ashton Court, a building which began life in the fifteenth century or thereabouts and has been growing ever since. Until recent years Ashton Park, one of the oldest enclosed parks in England (it being first fenced in in 1391), was the home of the Smyth family, who had been there since Elizabethan times. The countryside here is both hilly and well-wooded, and deer browse under the trees. Much property in the vicinity is attached to the University of Bristol, notably Long Ashton Research Station, which is concerned with research into fruit-growing, the development of new varieties of fruit and, appropriately for Somerset, the making of cider.

Other villages on this southern side of the Avon, such as Bishopsworth and Whitchurch, are now more or less swallowed by the outwards surge of Bristol. In mediaeval times, when Bristol was a port small enough to be contained by walls, the Avon was a convenient county boundary, but that time is past. It seems inevitable, though rather sad for those of us who treasure the past as well as the present, that a new county of Avon should be established, with the river Avon as its main artery rather than its frontier. This is happening at the time of writing, in 1974, and Somerset is losing a large slice of its north-western territory. Whatever our administrators and politicians may say, however, those who were born and live in the lost lands will always regard themselves as belonging to Somerset.

10. Plants, Birds, Beasts and People

Somerset is a naturalist's Eldorado. The astonishing diversity of geological structure is naturally reflected in the plants which clothe the rocks and in the birds, animals, insects and other life which live on them. While we have no internationally attractive nature reserve of the quality of the Camargue or the Dobrudja, it would be difficult to find an area of equal size which exhibits such a wide range of habitats with their respective fauna and flora as Somerset from Ilchester to Exmoor, from Yeovil to Yatton.

For natural history recording the county is divided into seven districts: north Somerset; east Somerset; Mendip; central Somerset; Taunton; south Somerset; and Exmoor.

As an example of the contrasts that may be found in the space of a few miles, let us look at some of the differences between the last two districts, as illustrated by a recent bird report of the Somerset Archaeological and Natural History Society. South Somerset comprises the region around Yeovil, Crewkerne, Ilminster and Ilchester and is a fairly typical area of hills, meadows, woods, coombes and some marshes. Exmoor has wild moorland, some of the highest hills in southern England and a long coastline that ranges from stupendous cliffs in the west to the mudflats of Bridgwater Bay.

During 1972 the following breeding species, which were not found nesting in south Somerset, were recorded for the Exmoor region: Shelduck, Fulmar, Merlin, Red Grouse, Black Grouse, Tree Pipit, Rock Pipit, Dipper, Wood Warbler, Pied Flycatcher, Stonechat, Wheatear, Redstart, Ring Ousel, Redpoll and Raven. In or over the Bristol Channel off the Exmoor coast numbers of Terns (Common, Arctic, Sandwich and one Little) were seen, also Razorbills, Guillemots and Kittiwakes. On the other hand, south Somerset has records for Nightingales, Corn Buntings, Great Crested Grebes and Tufted Duck which are not recorded for the Exmoor region. South Somerset has numerous records of ducks of nearly all the British inland species on its reservoirs, notably Sutton Bingham. The Exmoor coast, on the other hand, has an Eider Duck record, and there were more farther up the Severn, off Brean Down.

The reservoirs naturally attract large numbers of waterfowl in winter and are much visited by ornithologists. Most important of these waters are Chew Valley, Blagdon, Cheddar, the Barrow Gurney group, Durleigh, Sutton Bingham, Clatworthy, Blagdon Hill group, Hawkridge, Nutscale and Chard. Chew Valley reservoir is enormous, covering 1,200 acres and can be studied from public roads. Cheddar is a very deep reservoir with bare banks and so attracts only exclusive aquatic birds, such as diving ducks, coot and terns, as a rule, though storm-driven birds from the Channel often take refuge there. Some of the other reservoirs, with more shelter and shallower, muddy margins, attract hosts of waders in the migration seasons and in winter.

Enormous numbers of birds from the north and east travel as far as Somerset in autumn and go no farther. The flooded levels of central Somerset offer ideal feeding-grounds, but they are so extensive that the birds are often well dispersed. After heavy local flooding large flocks of gulls, fieldfares, starlings, rooks, lapwings and sometimes golden plover may be seen feeding on a detritus which includes hosts of insects drowned by the floods. Looking again at the 1972 Somerset Bird Report, we see counts of 3,000 or more Lapwings in at least five localities, with 10,000 on King's Sedgemoor in December. In the same area more than 16,000 Black-headed Gulls were estimated on flood water also in December. In winter about 12,000 Black-headed Gulls and 5,000 Common Gulls were roosting by Chew Valley Reservoir. Huge starling roosts are also a feature of the county. Some less common birds also occur in considerable numbers in winter. The 1972 Report has records of over 1,000 Snipe on Somerton Moor in February and around the same number by Cheddar Reservoir in December; 1,500 Golden Plover at Minehead in December; over 1,000 Dunlin at four separate coastal localities in winter; 1,800 Knot by the Axe estuary in February; over 1,000 Manx Shearwater in the Channel off Brean Down in spring; 3,500 Wigeon on Tealham Moor in February; and 652 Black-tailed Godwit at Stert on September migration.

There are about a dozen heronries in the county, the largest at Swell Wood, near Fivehead, which contained 58 nests in 1972. In a survey made in 1933/4 there were 669 rookeries with a total of 35,643 nests, and it is thought that the overall population has not altered much. Although Peregrine Falcons, which once nested in many Somerset localities, have become rare, Buzzards are quite common and have within the past 40 or 50 years extended their range eastwards to the farthest edge of the county. So too have Grey Wagtails, though Red-backed Shrikes and Wrynecks have become very uncommon.

Turning to mammals, Somerset has all three British species of deer. Exmoor has its herds of Red Deer, with an estimated population of 500 to 700, and there is another self-contained herd on the Quantocks. The Exmoor deer seem to be spreading eastwards to recolonize the Brendons. Roe deer are commonest in the southern and eastern parts of the county, having spread over from Dorset, where they were reintroduced, after becoming virtually extinct in England, in the nineteenth century. Fallow deer are well dispersed, though mostly in parks. There are also a few Sika, or Japanese deer, introduced to parks.

Foxes are abundant and badgers fairly plentiful. The status of otters is difficult to determine, as these animals travel considerable distances in a short time, but they are widespread in the central levels, where it is not uncommon to see otter tracks in the mud. Stoats in general are fairly common, and weasels more so. There are far too many escaped mink about for the welfare of both wild nesting birds and of domestic poultry. In woodland districts grey squirrels are also abundant nest-robbers. Predictably in a countryside so well provided with waterways, water-voles are quite plentiful. Rabbits are staging some recovery after the epidemic of myxomatosis from 1953 onwards, and hares are not uncommon.

All kinds of water creatures are abundant in the levels. There are frogs, toads and newts in the pools and marshes, dragon-flies and demoiselle flies flitting around the reeds, and plenty of fish, though nearly all coarse ones, in the rivers and canals. Pike, perch and eels are abundant there, but salmon and trout require the clearer water of upland streams. Both are found in the rivers of the western sector of the county. There are many angling clubs in Somerset, fishing most of the waterways and reservoirs. A local delicacy is elvers, or young eels, which come up the Parret and Severn with the spring tides and are scooped out by the bucketful, to be served in a kind of fishy omelette.

In times past, of course, Somerset had a much more extensive fauna. In the chapter on Mendip we have taken note of some of the fearsome mammals which were contemporary with the prehistoric men who lived in the caves there. Within historical times wild cat, beaver, wild boar and marten were all present, and probably wolves and bears as well. In the list of birds the bones of which have been found in Mendip caverns and the débris of the lake villages of Meare and Glastonbury we find pelicans, whit-tailed eagle, ptarmigan, golden eagle, crane, osprey, eagle owl and several species of geese and godwit.

In our Introduction we observed that Somerset was a land of apple trees, and its orchards are indeed one of the most noticeable features of the lowland parts of the shire. They provide habitats for many interesting birds, notably woodpeckers, chaffinches and gold-finches, and it is rather surprising that wrynecks, which love old orchards, should have become so scarce, for although many of the older orchards have been destroyed or have disappeared through neglect there are still plenty left. In them can be found some of the oldest varieties of apple, such as Tom Putt, Kingston Black (a cider apple) and Codlin.

The commonest of all trees in lowland Somerset is undoubtedly the elm, which stands in ranks in almost every hedgerow and forms towering clumps wherever it can find elbow room. At the time of writing Dutch elm disease is running its disastrous course through the Somerset elms, and what the landscape will look like when the epidemic is over is unpleasant to contemplate. Willows of various species, alders and poplars are abundant on the marshy levels, by channels where marsh marigolds, irises and loosestrife bloom. Many of the gorges and lane cuttings that are frequent in the limestone country are completely overhung by great trees, often beech, syca-more and horse chestnut, and the rocky outcrops are festooned with trailing ivy and decorated with ferns, especially hart's-tongue. The sunnier parts of the lanes sparkle in spring with bluebells, pink campions, celandines and a host of bright blossoms. Many church-yards have very ancient yews, and Dulverton possesses an unusually massive and venerable sycamore, known as The Belfry Tree.

Fine parks, mostly laid out by eighteenth-century landowners, abound in Somerset, and in more recent times the Forestry Commission has been adding to the arboreal wealth of the county by large plantations of conifers, particularly in the forest of Neroche.

In the West, the lowland elms are replaced by hillside coverts of scrub oaks, by the beech belts of Exmoor, and on the moors by rowan and birch. 17,000 acres of the Exmoor area are under trees, however, much of them excellent softwoods. Some of the largest oaks in England are in Nettlecombe Deer Park, on the northern slopes of Brendon Hills. In the villages around Porlock numbers of fine walnut trees perhaps owe their origin to plantings during the Napoleonic wars, with a view to providing a future supply of gunstocks.

Among the rarer plants of Somerset are the single peony which, as already mentioned, is found only on the island of Steepholm, the white rock-rose, abundant on Brean Down and hardly anywhere else, and the Cheddar pink. A wide variety of orchids is found in the county, some such as the greenwinged and marsh orchids on the fens and some, such as the twayblade and spotted, on the limestone hills.

In the matter of farm livestock, Somerset has only a few specialities. Nowadays the ubiquitous Friesian is the supreme dairy cow, though there are some herds of the Ayrshires, Guernseys, Jerseys and Dairy Shorthorns. The ruby-red Devon territory overspills into Somerset in the south and west. Two or three centuries ago, however, Somerset had a special type, if not breed, of its own. Old agricultural writers make frequent references to the Somerset 'sheeted cattle'. These were red cows 'with a white sheet thrown over their barrels; head, neck shoulders and hind parts being uncovered'. About them a Professor David Low wrote, in 1842:

'The sheeted cattle has existed in the same parts of England from time immemorial. The red colour of the hair has a light yellow tinge, and the white colour passes like a sheet over the whole body. The individuals are sometimes horned but more frequently polled. The cows are hardy, docile and well suited to the dairy. The beef of the oxen is of good quality and well marbled. The breed has become rare, which is to be regretted, since it is much better suited to the dairy than others which have been adopted.'

Prints survive of paintings made in 1841 of three sheeted cattle. Two polled ones were from the herd of a Mr John Weir of West Camel, and a horned one belonged to Sir John Phelips of Montacute. The only sheeted cattle now left in Britain are the Belted Galloways, a beef breed from the Scottish lowlands.

Another Somerset breed once very plentiful in the cheese-making areas in the east of the county was the Old Gloucestershire. This was a dairy-type animal, generally of a deep chocolate brown or black colour with a white 'finch' marking along the spine and tail. The globules of its milk were specially suitable for cheese-making. A few herds of this breed still survive—all, I think, in Gloucestershire.

The plentiful sheep which graze the orchards, meadows and hills of Somerset in spring and summer are mostly crossbreeds nowadays. There is little information about the type of sheep on which the great wool trade, and probably the cheese industry, of the Middle Ages was based. Two present-day breeds of sheep, however, seem to be more or less indigenous to Somerset (and Devon). One is the Exmoor Horn, a breed which has lived on Exmoor from time immemorial. The other, the Devon Closewool, is based on crosses between the Devon Longwool and Exmoor Horn and is at home on the more fertile lands south of the Moor.

Exmoor has another breed of domestic animal in the Exmoor pony, which its breeders claim has lived on Exmoor since at least the Bronze Age. The manor of Brendon alone had 104 brood mares at the time of the Domesday Book. These splendid little ponies still thrive and are in great demand, both in Britain and overseas, especially America. Their welfare is looked after by an alert Exmoor Pony Society.

Any treatise on the natural history of a region should properly include the human inhabitants, who, after all, represent just another species. The ancestry of Somerset folk is extraordinarily mixed. As we have seen in our surveys of various periods of history, in Somerset there has never been a wholesale replacement of one race by another, as happened on several occasions farther east. Iberian and

Celt, Saxon and Dane, Fleming, Welshman and Jew, were all peace-ably absorbed. And as has been observed in other connections, when fraternity broke down maternity usually succeeded.

It is futile therefore to look for a Somerset type. Philologists attempt from the study of place-names to determine which were the districts where Celtic influence predominated longest, but that is no clue to the character of the present inhabitants. It is true, however, that Somerset families tend to stay put in their homeland. To take as an example three families which take their name from Somerset villages—Chedzoy, Montacute and Podimore. In the massive London telephone directories I find only three Chedzoys, eight Podimores (spelt 'Podmore', if that is the same name) and no Montacutes. Yet in the Taunton directory are 22 Chedzoys (as well as two Chedzeys), 19 Pattemores (the same name), and 10 Montacutes.

Perhaps the best distinguishing feature of the people of Somerset is their dialect. For the most part it is based on old Saxon (once the royal tongue of England) and differs only in minor respects from the dialects of Dorset and Wiltshire. The Devon dialect shows distinct differences, and the dialect used in the Exmoor area tends to be nearer that of Devon than of Somerset east of the Parret. In Devon speech, for instance, 'us' is frequently used instead of 'we' as the nominative first person plural. . . .

> 'Cream of the West,
> The vust, the best,
> The pick o' the bunch us be.'

The Shibboleth of the Somerset tongue runs as follows:

'Thee cassen zee as well as thee cou'st, ca'st? And if thee coo'st thee oosen!'

Apart from the adoption of the old Puritan custom of using 'thee' instead of 'thou', this is pure Anglo-Saxon. The speaker is using the old second person singular instead of the plural 'you', which is the habit our slipshod age has fallen into. Translated, the phrase is:

'Thou canst not see as well as thou couldst, canst thou? And if thou couldst, thou wouldst not!'

The pronunciation 'oosen' typifies the habit of dropping the 'w'. As we noted in Chapter 2, an old way of spelling 'Selwood' as 'Seluud' was setting down phonetically just what Somerset folk would say. 'Wood' is 'ood'. Somerset dialect also abounds in 'v's and 'z's. 'Furze', for instance, becomes 'vuzz'. A 'scythe' is a 'zive'.

Some of the old Anglo-Saxon names strike us as being amusing tongue-twisters. The authors of *1066 and All That* had fun with Aethelfrith and Thrithelthrolth and suchlike names. Somerset people know that the 'th' is pronounced thickly, like 'dh', not like 'th' in 'thin'—which makes pronunciation much easier. The diphthong 'Ae' is still used. 'Alfred' is still pronounced 'Eelfred'. I have often in times past heard old Somerset preachers in their prayers appeal to 'Yealmighty God'. And I think that those Americans who refer to Athens as 'Ayethens' probably descended from Somerset migrants.

Ilchester, say its older inhabitants, was never pronounced as spelt. It was 'Yelchester', or 'Ealchester' or even 'Zelchester'. Another trick of speech is to transpose the vowel and the 'r' when 'r' comes after 'b' or 'p'. Thus 'apron' becomes 'yeappern'. And Bridgwater as 'Burdgewater' comes near to revealing its true derivation.

In considering dialect this chapter could be prolonged indefinitely. For more than 40 years now I have been writing a column of country notes in the *Western Gazette*, and whenever I touch upon the subject of dialect letters from readers arrive by the score. To pick a few words at random that have brought me correspondence recently :

Tunigar is a funnel, used particularly of a funnel for pouring cider into barrels.

Swale means to burn or scorch, used particularly of burning the parings from hedge-banks or for singeing a pig.

Yarks are leather straps for fastening the old type of corduroy trousers just below the knee, to keep the bottoms from dragging in the mud.

Gladdigloasters are woodlice. So are *bakers* and *barleybuts* and *Granfer Croogurs*.

To shriggle is to strip the last peas off the haulm.

A *nesteltripe* or *darl* is the last ne'er-do-well pig of a litter; also called a *runt*.

A *tallet* is a hay-loft.

Eddish is the aftermath of grass, after mowing.

Vlonkers are the sparks that fly upwards.

Shrammed is shivering with cold.

Vamous means excellent or excellently ('We be gettin' on vamous, her and me').

A *yealm* or *yellum* is a thatch bundle.

To dudder is to confuse.

Atterclaps means consequences.

To glutch is to swallow greedily.

Shirkin means lazy.

To plim means to swell.

The list could extend for pages. As a conclusion, here is an old Somerset toast. (Incidentally, it is interesting to note that although the 'w' is usually dropped from words such as 'wood' and 'would' it is generally added to certain words beginning with a vowel, notably to 'old', which becomes 'wold' or 'woold'.)

'Here's to theas woold ouse. May the hroof auven never vall in, and may they wot's in en never vall out!'

Index